CAVEN

Family Law

Third Edition

Cavendish Publishing Limited

London • Sydney • Portland, Oregon

Third edition first published in Great Britain 2003 by
Cavendish Publishing Limited, The Glass House,
Wharton Street, London WC1X 9PX, United Kingdom
Telephone: + 44 (0)20 7278 8000   Facsimile: + 44 (0)20 7278 8080
Email: info@cavendishpublishing.com
Website: www.cavendishpublishing.com

Published in the United States by Cavendish Publishing
c/o International Specialized Book Services,
5824 NE Hassalo Street, Portland,
Oregon 97213-3644, USA

Published in Australia by Cavendish Publishing (Australia) Pty Ltd
3/303 Barrenjoey Road, Newport, NSW 2106, Australia

© Cavendish Publishing Ltd 2003

All rights reserved. No part of this publication may be reproduced, stored in a
retrieval system, or transmitted, in any form or by any means, electronic, mechanical,
photocopying, recording, scanning or otherwise, without the prior permission in
writing of Cavendish Publishing Limited, or as expressly permitted by law, or under
the terms agreed with the appropriate reprographics rights organisation. Enquiries
concerning reproduction outside the scope of the above should be sent to the
Rights Department, Cavendish Publishing Limited, at the address above.

You must not circulate this book in any other binding or cover
and you must impose the same condition on any acquirer.

Cataloguing in Publication Data
Data available

ISBN 1-85941-768-X

1 3 5 7 9 10 8 6 4 2

Typeset by Phoenix Photosetting, Chatham, Kent
Printed and bound in Great Britain

Contents

1. Nullity — 1
2. Divorce — 15
3. Ancillary Relief — 31
4. Family Homes and Domestic Violence — 53
5. Children I — 73
6. Children II — 97

1 Nullity

Although fewer than 1% of marriages are now terminated by nullity petitions today, examiners still require a knowledge of this area.

Nullity falls into two categories – void and voidable marriages. Each area has its own concepts and grounds for its existence.

Void marriages

There are social and public policy reasons as to why the marriage should not exist, as illustrated by the grounds contained in s 11 of the Matrimonial Causes Act (MCA) 1973. Because of public policy considerations, void marriages are void *ab initio* and the decree granted is declaratory but necessary to gain financial provisions. Also, third parties can challenge the validity of the marriage. There are no special defences.

Marriages celebrated after 31 July 1971 will be void on the following grounds.

Section 11(a)(i)

The parties to the marriage are within the prohibited degrees of relationship: either blood relations (consanguinity) or non-blood relations (affinity).

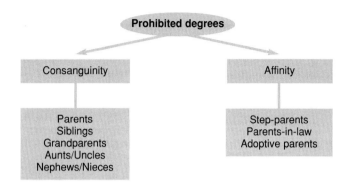

Section 11(a)(ii)

Either party is under the age of 16. However, if both parties are domiciled abroad at the time of the marriage, the marriage will be recognised as valid if it is recognised as valid in the country in which it was celebrated.

If either party is aged over 16 but under 18, then consent is required from certain people:

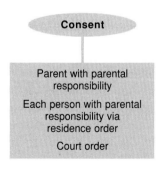

1 Nullity

However, if this consent is lacking, the marriage will not be void unless the parents have publicly objected to the banns, thereby voiding them. An application can also be made to the High Court, county court or magistrates' court to obtain consent if the parents cannot give consent due to absence or inaccessibility.

Section 11(a)(iii)

The parties have intermarried in disregard of certain requirements as to the formation of marriage.

Publicity has been deemed necessary to prevent clandestine marriages, as illustrated by the existing rules, which are complex and are dealt with here only in outline.

Formalities for weddings

Cavendish LawCards: Family Law

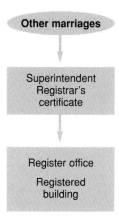

When there are defects in the formalities, the marriage will only be void if they are brought about 'knowingly and wilfully' by both parties.

VOID
- No certificate/licence
- No banns/notice
- Banns not published properly
- Public objection to banns
- Over three months since banns
- Celebrant not qualified
- Building not approved/referred to in licence

Lack of consent: not necessarily void

Section 11(b)

At the time of the marriage, either party was already lawfully married.

This sub-section requires the parties to satisfy the definition of marriage contained in *Hyde v Hyde* (1866), that is, 'the voluntary union for life of one man and one woman to the exclusion of all others'. In *Whiston v Whiston* (1995), the woman had committed bigamy, knowing that her first husband was still alive.

Maples v Maples (1987) illustrates that if a party has entered a valid marriage, then, in order to terminate that marriage and be able to enter another, the termination must also be valid.

Section 11(c)

The parties are not respectively male and female. The cases arising in this area normally concern a party who has undergone a sex change.

UK	EUROPE
Corbett v Corbett (1970)	*Rees v UK* (1990)
Bellinger v Bellinger (2001)	*Cossey v UK* (1991)
	B v France (1992)
	Goodwin v UK (2000)

The approach in England and Wales was to treat a transsexual as being of their original birth sex, even if they had undergone full reassignment surgery, as the tests to be used related to chromosomal structures, etc, as decided in *Corbett*. Following the European Court of Human Rights' decision in *Goodwin*, this will no longer be the case. Transsexuals who have completed reassignment surgery must be treated as their new sex for the purposes of marriage.

Section 11(d)

In the case of a polygamous marriage entered into outside England and Wales, either party was, at the time of the marriage, domiciled in England or Wales.

Section 47 of the MCA 1973 allows matrimonial relief or a declaration concerning the validity of a marriage entered into under a law allowing polygamy (matrimonial relief includes nullity, divorce, judicial separation and matters relating to maintenance provisions). However, there have been cases where s 11(d) has not applied.

In *Radwan v Radwan (No 2)* (1973), the husband was domiciled in Egypt and married his first wife, an Egyptian domiciled woman, in Cairo. He later married his second wife, an English domiciled woman, in Paris, intending to enter into a polygamous marriage according to Egyptian law and to live in Egypt. They did live in Egypt, but later moved to, and became domiciled in, England. The second wife later petitioned for divorce.

The court held that, as the second marriage was valid in Egypt and they had intended to live there, it was valid in England. The court said that s 11(d) did not apply.

In *Hussain v Hussain* (1982), even though there was a potentially polygamous marriage, both parties had no capacity to marry again and s 11(d) did not apply; therefore, the marriage was valid.

Voidable marriages

Voidable marriages are defective, but it is for the parties involved to decide whether they will end the marriage. The marriage will continue until it is avoided by way of a decree.

When a voidable marriage ends

Section 16 of the MCA 1973 states that a decree of nullity granted after 31 July 1971 on the ground that a marriage is voidable will only annul the marriage with respect to any time after the decree has been made absolute. The marriage will be treated as if it had existed up to that time, notwithstanding the decree.

> *Ward v Secretary of State for Social Services* (1990)
>
> *Pike v Pike* (1994)

The grounds for voidability of marriages formed after 31 July 1971 are contained in s 12 of the MCA 1973.

Section 12(a)

The marriage has not been consummated owing to the incapacity of either party to consummate it.

Section 12(b)

The marriage has not been consummated owing to the wilful refusal of the respondent to consummate it.

The difference in the wording of these grounds shows that, under s 12(a), a party can petition on his own incapacity but, under s 12(b), he cannot petition on his own wilful refusal.

Consummation occurs as soon as parties have sexual intercourse after the marriage. Sexual intercourse before marriage does not amount to consummation. The degree of sexual intercourse required was defined in *D v A* (1845). This was illustrated in *W v W* (1967), where it was stated that, as the husband was incapable of sustaining an erection, consummation did not occur.

Wilful refusal

This is defined in *Horton v Horton* (1947) as 'a settled and definite decision come to without just excuse'.

This can arise in a number of ways, such as a psychological problem which does not amount to incapacity or the refusal to undergo an operation to remedy a physical defect preventing consummation. However, it must meet the definition, that is, it must be a settled and definite decision without just cause.

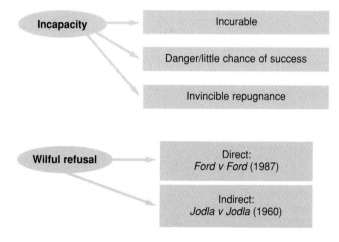

1 Nullity

Section 12(c)

Lack of consent: either party did not validly consent, whether in consequence of duress, mistake, unsoundness of mind or otherwise.

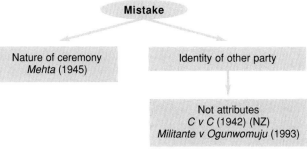

Unsoundness of mind

```
        Unsoundness of mind

Either party's failure to understand nature of marriage
             at the time of marriage
```

There is a presumption that, when a party enters into a marriage, he is capable of doing so and the burden of proof lies with the respondent.

Duress

Duress is said to be fear which is so overbearing that the element of free consent is absent.

In *Szechter v Szechter* (1971), it was said that it must amount to:

> ... a genuine and reasonably held fear caused by the threat of immediate danger (for which the party himself is not responsible) to life, limb or liberty, so that the constraint destroys the reality of consent.

Duress

- Objective test?
- Subjective test:
  Threat to life and liberty not literal
  Better view:
  Hirani v Hirani (1982)

It is generally accepted that a subjective test is to be applied in this situation, that is, 'has the petitioner been affected by the pressure?', not 'would an ordinary person of firm standing be affected?' (*Scott v Sebright* (1886)). This pressure need not be in relation to life, limb or liberty, but must be sufficient to overbear the will of the person and destroy the reality of consent, as in *Hirani v Hirani* (1982), where social ostracism was seen as duress. In Scotland the courts have frequently applied this subjective test to arranged marriages where one of the parties has gone through the marriage ceremony due to family pressures and possible ostracism.

Section 12(d)

This sub-section deals with a party suffering from a mental disorder. In this situation, a party can give valid consent and, because of this, the marriage cannot be avoided by s 12(c).

However, the party may not be fit for marriage because of the mental disorder.

The mental disorder, which can be continuous or intermittent, must be within the Mental Health Act 1983.

Section 12(e)

At the time of marriage, the respondent was suffering from VD in a communicable form.

Section 12(f)

At the time of the marriage, the respondent was pregnant by some person other than the petitioner.

Bars when marriages are voidable

If the situation arises where the respondent wishes to prevent a decree of nullity being granted, the use of s 13 of the MCA 1973 must be considered.

Section 13(1)

The court shall not grant a decree of nullity on the ground that a marriage is voidable if the respondent satisfies the court that:

- the petitioner, with knowledge that it was open to him to have the marriage avoided, so conducted himself in relation to the respondent as to lead the respondent reasonably to believe that he would not seek to do so; and
- it would be unjust to the respondent to grant the decree.

Knowledge : Conduct : Unjust

Section 13(2) and (3)

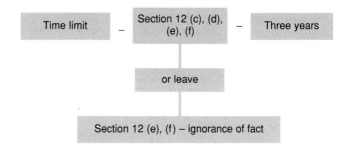

Section 13(4)

This allows leave to be granted for proceedings to be instituted out of time if the court:

- ○ is satisfied that the petitioner has, at some time during that period, suffered from a mental disorder within the Mental Health Act 1983; and
- ○ considers that, in all the circumstances of the case, it would be just to grant leave for the institution of proceedings.

Children

Section 41 of the MCA 1973 applies to cases of nullity. This section requires the court to consider whether it should use its powers under the Children Act 1989 in relation to any children involved in the case.

Financial provision

As a consequence of gaining a decree of nullity, whether due to the marriage being void or voidable, the parties are entitled to any of the financial and property orders available under the MCA 1973 that the court feels it appropriate to make. The orders will take effect on the granting of the decree.

The criteria that apply to the making of these orders are set out in s 25 of the MCA 1973 and are considered further in Chapter 3.

2 Divorce

Matrimonial Causes Act 1973

```
Section 3(1)
absolute bar on divorce
within one year
         │
Section 1(1)
irretrievable breakdown –
sole ground
         │
Section 1(2)
irretrievable breakdown to be shown
by one or more of five facts
         │
Section 1(1) and (2)
must be satisfied
         │
If one or more facts shown, court
must grant petition unless satisfied
irretrievable breakdown not present
```

Adultery and intolerability

Section 1(2)(a)

The elements of the definition of adultery must be known.

Adultery

Voluntary sexual intercourse between a married person and a person of the opposite sex, who may or may not be married and who is not the other person's spouse.

The act must be voluntary (*Redpath v Redpath and Milligan* (1950)).

The degree of sexual intercourse required for adultery is that some degree of penetration is achieved (*Dennis v Dennis* (1955)). (This can be compared with the degree of sexual intercourse required for consummation, that is, 'ordinary and complete'.)

Intolerability

Adultery is considered to be a serious matrimonial offence and, as such, a standard of proof higher than the normal civil standard of proof is required (*Bastable v Bastable* (1968)).

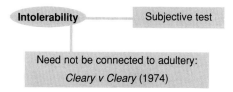

Reconciliation provision: s 2(1) and (2)

Cohabitation of over six months after becoming aware of adultery 'destroys' the fact.

Behaviour

Section 1(2)(b)

This fact is normally referred to as 'unreasonable behaviour'. However, the aspect of 'unreasonableness' must be considered in relation to whether or not the petitioner is expected to live with the respondent, not to the standard of behaviour.

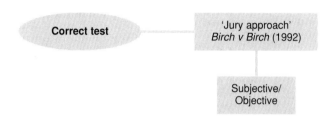

The test applied must have both elements. A subjective view should be taken of the petitioner's character and personality and an objective view of whether it is reasonable to expect her to live with the respondent: *Livingstone-Stallard v Livingstone-Stallard* (1974).

Reconciliation provisions

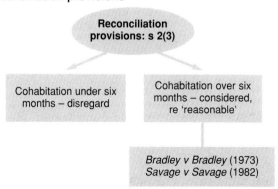

Desertion

Section 1(2)(c)

There are said to be four requirements to prove the fact of desertion.

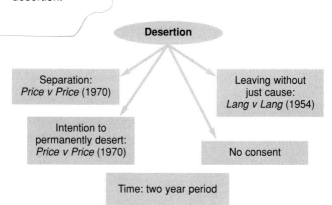

Termination of desertion

Absolute defences:

- the granting of a decree of judicial separation or a valid separation agreement. These are seen as supervening consent;
- the refusal of a reasonable offer of reconciliation without just cause, for example, a party offering reconciliation but attaching unreasonable conditions. In *Hutchinson v Hutchinson* (1963), there was to be no sexual intercourse: the husband was going to refuse sexual intercourse on the wife's return. This was held to be an

unreasonable condition and the husband was held to be in constructive desertion;
- resumption of cohabitation would amount to returning to a state of affairs where desertion would not have been found originally.

Discretionary defences

- Petitioner's implied consent to the separation by taking action to prevent the other spouse returning.
- Petitioner unsuccessfully petitioning for divorce or nullity on other grounds.

Separation

Section 1(2)(d): two years' separation and respondent consents.

Section 1(2)(e): five years' separation.

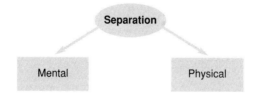

The recognition of the marriage being at an end can be made unilaterally and need not be communicated to the other spouse. It is clear that this could cause hardship, and the court will require evidence which shows when such a decision was reached. This could be by way of oral evidence, a letter or the ending of regular visits. However, if the court only has the oral evidence of the petitioner, it will treat such evidence with caution and look at the surrounding circumstances to see if there are any other indications as to when the period began.

Separate households

Section 2(6) states that a husband and wife shall be treated as living apart unless they are living with each other in the same household. This means that we have to consider the question of separate households under the same roof.

The essential element is that it can be shown that there has been a change in the nature of the relationship. This can best be illustrated by considering the cases of *Fuller v Fuller* (1973) and *Mouncer v Mouncer* (1972). In *Fuller* the relationship changed to that of landlady and lodger, whereas in *Mouncer* the parties shared community of living (meals etc) and acted as a 'family'.

Consent

The essential difference in the facts of these cases concerns the requirement of consent by the respondent in s 1(2)(d) only.

The petitioner has the burden of showing that the respondent has consented in the proper manner. This consent must be expressed and is normally given via a signed statement. The respondent should be given sufficient information to enable him to give a proper consent to the decree.

The court will not imply any element of consent (*McGill v Robson* (1972)).

As with all matters of consent, there must be capacity (*Mason v Mason* (1972)). Again, it is for the petitioner to show that the respondent has this capacity if there is any doubt.

The respondent can withdraw his consent at any time prior to the decree nisi (r 2.10(2) of the Family Proceedings Courts Rules 1991). Also, under s 10(1) of the MCA 1973, the respondent may apply to the court at any time before decree absolute for the decree nisi to be rescinded if he can satisfy the court that he was misled by the petitioner, whether intentionally or not, on any matter which he took into consideration in giving his consent.

Once the five year separation under s 1(2)(e) has been proven to exist and has been acknowledged by the respondent, the respondent may not then attempt to petition or cross petition for divorce on any other fact (*Parsons v Parsons* (1975)).

Time requirements

These are strictly applied, as shown by *Warr v Warr* (1975), and do not include the day of separation.

Reconciliation

Reconciliation in under six months

Time spent on reconciliation does not count towards the 2 or 5 year period and acts as an interruption to the time clock

Reconciliation in over 6 months

Stops the time clock completely – any period of separation before the reconciliation cannot be counted. The parties must start the time clock again and separate for 2 or 5 years

Provisions affecting the granting of decrees

Section 5

This defence is available only in cases based on fact (s 1(2)(e)).

- Respondent could suffer grave financial *or* other hardship caused by the granting of the decree *and* it would in all the circumstances be wrong to dissolve the marriage.
- All elements need to be satisfied.

The application is made prior to the decree nisi and the court will consider all the circumstances of the case, including the conduct of the parties, their interests and the interests of any children or others.

Grave financial hardship

Usually arises through loss of pensions for older wives, although note the extent of the court's powers to deal with the issue of pensions in Chapter 3.

- 'Grave' – ordinary meaning applied to all types of hardship – *Reiterbund v Reiterbund* (1974); *Rukat v Rukat* (1975)
- Subjective view taken re particular marriage but objective view taken of 'grave' – *Rukat v Rukat* (1975); *Mathias v Mathias* (1972)
- Hardship must be caused by the granting of the decree – *Talbot v Talbot* (1971)

Other payments may be made to compensate:

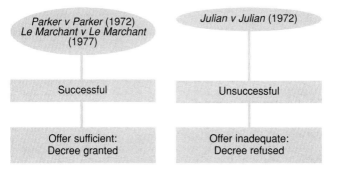

Wrong to dissolve the marriage

Even if the respondent can show 'grave financial or other hardship', it is also necessary to show that it would be wrong to dissolve the marriage. In *Brickell v Brickell* (1973), the respondent's wife was able to show grave financial hardship but, because of her behaviour in spying on her husband and causing the failure of his business, it was held that it would not be wrong to dissolve the marriage. The decree was granted.

Section 10

In cases based on the facts in s 1(2)(d) and (e), the respondent can apply to the court for consideration of his financial provision on divorce. This provision is contained in s 10(2) of the MCA 1973. Section 10(3) empowers the court not to make the decree absolute unless it is satisfied that the petitioner need not make any financial provision or that the provision made is reasonable and fair or the best that can be made in the circumstances.

In reaching its decision the court will have regard to the criteria set out in s 25 of the MCA 1973 and covered in Chapter 3.

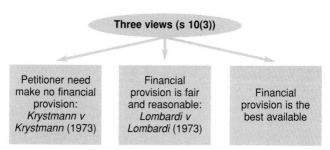

Garcia v Garcia (1992) – covers past and future provisions.

The court can delay the granting of the decree absolute if it is not satisfied.

Under s 10(4), the court can make the decree absolute, despite s 10(3), if the circumstances make it desirable to do so without delay or if it receives a satisfactory undertaking from the petitioner that he will make financial provision for the respondent that the court may approve.

The undertaking must not be vague, as the court must be able to enforce it. In the absence of specific proposals, the court will decide on an appropriate order.

Section 41

This provision applies to all divorces where there are children involved. It does not depend on the application of the respondent. Under this provision, the court shall consider if there are any children of the family concerned and, where there are such children, whether, in the light of any proposed arrangements for the welfare of those children, it should exercise any of its powers under the Children Act 1989 in respect of any of them.

The procedure in brief

The manner in which a divorce is obtained has led to criticism of the law. The 'special procedure', which applies to all but defended divorces, enables the parties to obtain their decree without the need to attend court, and with the court's role limited to scrutiny of the divorce documentation. The petitioner will be required to file at court the divorce petition, to which the respondent files a response. If there is no question of a defence or cross petition, the petitioner also swears an affidavit as to the evidence relied on to prove the irretrievable breakdown of the marriage and the fact from s 1(2) of the MCA 1973. The district judge, if happy with the nature of the documents, and that the evidence in the petition supports the fact, will grant decree nisi, and thereafter the petitioner can seek the decree absolute to finalise the divorce.

Criticisms of the present system

Over recent years, there has been growing dissatisfaction with the law concerning divorce in this country and the seemingly ever increasing number of divorces, which now stands at approximately 137,000 per annum, according to the Judicial Statistics for 2001. The main criticisms of the present system are that it:

- allows marriages to be ended too quickly and easily without the parties having to have regard to the consequences and effects on others of their actions;
- does little to try and preserve marriages that are in difficulty;

- does little to try to diminish any adverse effects or trauma suffered by the children of the family;
- increases the bitterness and hostility between the parties;
- is misleading and confusing;
- is open to abuse. Adultery and behaviour are used in approximately 80% of divorces, but often, false allegations are used to facilitate the granting of the divorce;
- can be used to distort the parties' bargaining positions, for example, where matters regarding children are being used as bargaining ploys.

(*Family Law: The Ground for Divorce*, Law Com No 192, 1990.)

The reforms suggested to overcome these difficulties were intended to:

- support and save marriages capable of being saved;
- enable those not 'saveable' to be dissolved with the minimum of distress, hostility and bitterness;
- encourage, as far as possible, the amicable resolution of matters concerning finance, housing, children and parties' responsibilities to each other;
- prevent or minimise the harm and distress to any children of the family during and after the divorce, and to promote the continued sharing of parental responsibility and other responsibilities or duties towards the children.

The legislation that was brought forward by the government, the Family Law Act (FLA) 1996, while containing some of the Law Commission aims, placed emphasis on the methods to be used to reduce hostility and bitterness, to reduce the cost to the parties and the taxpayer, and to trying to reduce divorce by ensuring that the parties were fully informed as to the nature of the process.

Part II of the FLA 1996 was intended to repeal the MCA 1973 on divorce, and to replace the special procedure. Crucial to the FLA's reform were the concepts of mediation, covered by Part III, and provision of information on divorce – the so called Information Meetings. The government piloted both the mediation and information meetings to ensure that implementation of the FLA would go smoothly and also to test the models of provision. The results of these pilots were not as expected. The information meeting study showed that whilst many attendees welcomed the information, the meetings increased the number of attendees who felt that divorce was likely, and that only 7% of those attending the meeting moved on to consider mediation. The study into mediation concluded that it did not help to save marriages, that it did not always save costs, and mediation did not always achieve resolution on all matters in dispute. As a consequence, the Lord Chancellor announced on 16 January 2001 that the changes to divorce planned under Part II were to be repealed. To date, this had not happened, even though some of the sections have been brought into force. It can only be assumed that this is a legislative oversight, or that these changes will at some stage be brought into force fully, albeit with possible amendment.

Mediation

Mediation was seen as integral to the new divorce process under the FLA 1996 and the intention to reduce the harmful and distressing effects of divorce. By enabling couples to reach their own arrangements as to the future, improve communications between them and increase the chances for co-operation in relation to children, the aim was to remove the adversarial nature of the MCA system. In addition, given that the resolution of disputes would be 'party led', this would also lead to a reduction in the amount of state funding used in paying lawyers. Mediation was also seen as being a method of reducing the number of divorces, since it would leave the door open to reconciliation. This confusion between the concepts of mediation and reconciliation was unfortunate, since mediation is not primarily focused on saving the marriage, but on helping move the parties forward into life as a divorced individual, and perhaps may explain the lack of take-up of mediation services. Additionally, the fact that legal advice would still be needed, if only to draw up the resulting agreement for ratification by the court, may have hindered the scale of mediation take-up since the parties may have preferred to stay with their lawyer, rather than deal with two different services.

Part III of the FLA operated to introduce mediation to the process of divorce by way of amendments to the Legal Aid Act 1988. This Act has since been repealed by the Access to Justice Act 1990, and the mediation requirements for family disputes are now found in the Funding Code, which sets out the detailed criteria for the granting of state funding under this latter Act. The Code sets out the nature of proceedings which will be subject to mediation in para 2.2, and this includes (*inter alia*) matters under:

- the MCA 1973;
- the Adoption Act 1976;
- the Children Act 1989 (Parts I, II and III); and
- the FLA (Part IV).

Hence, if a party to any of the specified 'family matters' requires state funding, they will have to be assessed for suitability for mediation as a means to resolve the dispute, rather than being granted state funding for purely legal representation. The Funding Code sets out the procedure to be applied, and also establishes the situations where an assessment for mediation suitability is not appropriate. An applicant for state funding will not be required to undergo a mediation assessment:

- if the proceedings are under s 37 MCA 1973;
- if the proceedings are under the Inheritance (Provision for Family and Dependants) Act 1975;
- where it is in the interests of justice that legal representation be granted as a matter of urgency and the criteria for emergency representation are satisfied;
- where there is no mediator available to the applicant or any party to the proceedings to hold the assessment meeting;
- where the mediator is satisfied that mediation is not suitable to the dispute because another party to the dispute is unwilling to attend an assessment meeting with a mediator to consider mediation;
- where family proceedings are already in existence and the client is a respondent to the proceedings and there are less than eight weeks to the court hearing date; and
- where the applicant has a reasonable fear of domestic abuse from a potential party to the mediation and is therefore unwilling and fearful of mediating with them. (Funding Code Procedure paras C 28 and C 29).

If the applicant does not fall within one of the above categories, they will have to attend a meeting with the mediator to see if the dispute is capable of mediation. In the event that the matter is suitable, the applicant will be granted state funding for the purposes of mediation, to include legal representation in the drawing up of any agreement following mediation. Should mediation be deemed unsuitable, the applicant will be considered for state funding for legal representation. Suitability will require consideration by the mediator carrying out the assessment of factors such as the nature of the dispute, the parties' attitudes and all the circumstances of the case.

As with the previous legal aid scheme, applicants will also be considered on their financial eligibility. If the applicant is required to contribute to their funding, this contribution will apply regardless of whether they are undergoing mediation, or are receiving legal advice. There also exists the statutory charge in relation to mediation. Hence where property is recovered or preserved for the state funded party as a result of mediation, a sum equal to the fees incurred will be a first charge on that property in favour of the Legal Services Commission (the body that now administers state funding).

Should mediation be deemed appropriate following the assessment meeting and then fail to resolve the issue, the applicant may request state funding for legal assistance. This request will require additional consideration of the reasons for the failure of mediation and whether the applicant behaved reasonably throughout the mediation. If mediation fails, it cannot be assumed that funding for legal advice will then be granted.

The efficacy of mediation compared to legal advice and representation has been considered by Gwynn Davis *et al*, *Monitoring Publicly Funded Family Mediation* (2000). While it was concluded that mediation does have a value, it is not always as cost effective as legal advice alone, nor does it achieve resolution of the dispute. Hence it may be questioned why all applicants for state-funding should be pushed in the direction of mediation. It is also worth noting that many mediators expect the client to have access to legal advice during mediation since a mediator cannot advise or suggest outcomes. If a client requires state funding for mediation, how will they then be able to afford a lawyer as well?

3 Ancillary Relief

The welfare of minor children of the family (s 25(1) of the MCA 1973)

Ancillary relief claims are those relating to the distribution of financial and property assets between the parties after divorce, nullity (where a decree has been sought) or judicial separation, and include claims for children. The statutory provisions are the same, regardless of the extent of those assets, but in many so called 'big money cases' the court's discretion is much wider.

MCA 1973: types of orders

> **Section 23**
> *Money orders*
>
> ⊃ Periodical payments
> ⊃ Secured periodical payments
> ⊃ Lump sums

Issues in relation to these orders

⊃ Secured orders will survive the death of the payer.
⊃ Both secured and unsecured periodical payments orders cease on the remarriage of the payee.
⊃ Periodical payments may be varied, up or down.
⊃ Periodical payments may be ordered to cease in the event of cohabitation.

- Lump sum orders provide money up front, therefore later remarriage is irrelevant.
- A lump sum can be ordered to be paid in instalments.
- A lump sum can be invested to provide income.

Section 24
Property orders

- Transfer of property
- Settlement of property
- Variation of a settlement
- Extinguish or reduce a settlement

Issues in relation to these orders

- Transfers of property interest may be coupled with a lump sum payment to compensate for the loss of a capital asset.
- The compensation may take the form of a charge over the property removing access to capital for one party.
- Maintenance for children may not be offset against a capital transfer.
- Settling property until a specified event (eg the children reaching 18) may delay the sale and division of equity too much, resulting in one or both of the parties being unable to rehome.
- A settlement linked to remarriage or cohabitation may impact negatively on any children.
- None of these orders is consistent with a clean break.

3 Ancillary Relief

Section 24A
Express power of sale

All property in which either or both parties have an interest

Available if court makes:
- secured periodical payments order (s 23)
- lump sum order (s 23)
- property adjustment order (s 24)

Issues in relation to these orders

- Promotes the clean break.
- Is certain.
- Normally suitable in big money cases or where couples do not have dependent children.

Considerations for the court

When dealing with ancillary relief claims, the court is required to look at a range of factors as set out in the MCA 1973. The court does, however, have a wide discretion in dealing with the matrimonial assets, and is not particularly interested in who brought what into the relationship (*Hanlon v The Law Society* (1981)).

General considerations

The clean break (s 25A)

The idea behind these provisions is to bring to an end any dependence or obligation between the parties as soon as is practicable, depending on the circumstances of the case.

The court has a duty to consider a 'clean break' in each case (*Barrett v Barrett* (1988)). It does not have to apply the provisions. It will look at the situation in three ways:

> *Section 25A(1)*
> Is a 'clean break' appropriate?
>
> *Attar v Attar (No 2)* (1985)
> *Suter v Suter and Jones* (1987)
> *Scallon v Scallon* (1990)
> *Gojkovic v Gojkovic* (1990)

> *Section 25A(2)*
> If so, can it be granted immediately or after a period of adjustment?
>
> *M v M* (1987)
> *Evans v Evans* (1990)

> *Section 25A(3)*
> If not, should it be dismissed and an order made preventing further application for periodical payments?
>
> Or, what type of orders from the range available are suitable?

The starting points

In exercising its discretion, the court often uses 'starting points' to assist in establishing what would be the appropriate distribution. A variety of approaches have been favoured by the courts.

3 Ancillary Relief

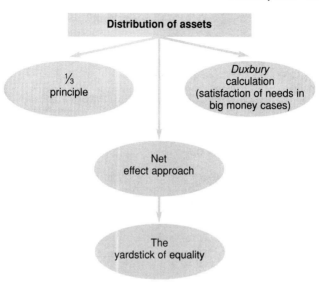

None of these starting points has to be used, although the consideration of the effect of the order is perhaps the most valuable, especially when taken with the yardstick of equality. The approach of the court will differ if it is a big money case – where there are sufficient assets to go round. The needs based approach, to which the *Duxbury* calculation is linked, focuses on big money cases – for instance, what does the wife need to live on, and how much capital, if invested, will produce that income. Following *White v White* (2000) this approach alone is not permitted. Now the courts must test this with the yardstick of equality to ensure that the parties are not being discriminated against, with the wife suffering as a result of being a home-maker rather than a business person. As can be seen, this would suggest that the ⅓ principle is also out of favour and should be discounted.

Specific considerations

The welfare of minor children of the family (s 25(1) of the MCA 1973)

The welfare of the children is not paramount under the MCA and will not override other considerations. However, it is the first and most important consideration (*Suter v Suter and Jones* (1987); *C v C (Financial Provision: Short Marriage)* (1997)).

Financial resources (s 25(2)(a))

The court will consider all the financial resources of the parties, including those likely to arise in the future. All sources of income will be considered.

> Court looks at the reality of the situation:
> *Hardy v Hardy* (1981); *Newton v Newton* (1990)

> The future must be considered – increase in earning capacity: *Mitchell v Mitchell* (1984)

> Potential payer must have means to pay:
> *Brown v Brown* (1981)

> New partner's income will only be considered as the effect of releasing more of the payer's resources for any orders to be made: *Martin v Martin* (1977); *Frary v Frary* (1993)

> The source of the resource: *White v White* (2000)

Financial needs, obligations and resources (s 25(2)(b))

As a direct corollary of income and resources, the court will consider what needs, obligations and responsibilities the parties will have now and in the future.

> Needs are assessed on a subjective basis:
> *Leadbeater v Leadbeater* (1985); *Dart v Dart* (1996)

> The party keeping the children will have future obligations until they become independent: *Mesher v Mesher* (1980)

> New families may need to be maintained as well as the former families. The court will attempt to balance the demands of both: *Stockford v Stockford* (1982)

Standard of living (s 25(2)(c))

When dealing with wealthy families, it is often possible for the court to settle matters without any significant drop in living standards. The court will consider the standard of living to which the parties have become accustomed and will seek to maintain that standard.

However, for the majority of couples, it is not possible for one household to become two without some drop in the standard of living. While the courts can try to apportion this reduction evenly, if there are dependent children this is not always feasible.

Ages and duration of marriage (s 25(2)(d))

The ages of the parties can have an effect on the orders made – it is much more common for young couples without children to be able to make a clean break from each other. If both are employed, the court may not need to make an order for maintenance/property adjustment at all.

However, in *C v C (Financial Provision: Short Marriage)* (1997), even though the marriage only lasted for nine months, the wife was given a large award because of the presence of a young child and her fragile state of health.

An older couple, especially with a long marriage, are likely to need more far reaching orders, particularly if the wife has given up a career to raise children and be a homemaker. She will be at an age where a career is unobtainable, and her devotion to the family needs compensating (*L v L* (2002)).

The courts will not normally equate marriage and cohabitation unless there is a significant degree of commitment: *Kokosinski v Kokosinski* (1980).

Physical or mental disability (s 25(2)(e))

> Allowances will be made for disability if it is possible to compensate by monetary means. If the disability deteriorates, then allowances will be made:
> *Sakkas v Sakkas* (1987)

Contributions to the family welfare (s 25(2)(f))

Contributions to the welfare of the family traditionally concentrate on the role played by the wife in raising the children. However, other types of contribution are just as relevant, and in particular, the contribution of building the family business and being an excellent money-maker are frequently cited. In *White v White* (2000) and *L v L* (2002) the courts have made clear that 'domestic contributions' should not be undervalued simply because they cannot be assessed/costed in the same way as economic activity.

```
                    Contributions can be
                     positive or negative
                    /                    \
         Positive                              Negative

  Gojkovic v Gojkovic                         E v E (1990)
     (No 2) (1991)
   Smith v Smith (1991)
   Cowan v Cowan (2001)
       L v L (2002)
```

Conduct that would be inequitable to disregard (s 25(2)(g))

The courts are reluctant to examine the parties' conduct: *E v E* (1990).

> Will be considered if 'both obvious and gross':
> *Kyte v Kyte* (1987)
> *Wachtel v Wachtel* (1973)

> Can also be conduct that is considered criminal:
> *Whiston v Whiston* (1995)
> *J v S-T (formerly J)* (1997)

> Does not have to be conduct that has contributed
> to the breakdown of the marriage:
> *Beach v Beach* (1995)

> Equally bad conduct by both parties will be disregarded:
> *Ash v Ash* (1972)

Loss of future benefit (s 25(2)(h))

The main benefit to be considered under this provision is the loss of pension entitlement as a spouse of the pension holder (*Parker v Parker* (1972); *Brooks v Brooks* (1995)). Following various amendments to the MCA 1973 the court has a range of options available to it:

- Set-off – the court can make an increased lump sum order or deal with the matrimonial property so as to give the non pension holder a greater share, thus compensating for the loss of pension benefits.
- Pension attachment orders – the court, under s 25B, C and D, can direct that a specified portion of the pension shall be paid to the spouse on the retirement of the pension holding spouse. No funds will be transferred prior to retirement. Assumes that the pension holding spouse will reach retirement age.
- Pension sharing orders – the court, under s 21A and s 24B, C and D, can direct that a specified portion of the pension shall be transferred immediately to the non pension holding spouse, to hold in their own pension fund. The fund may then be transferred to other pension providers, additional contributions added and payments will commence on the retirement of the recipient spouse.

However, even though these orders are available, any order will be at the court's discretion and will only be made after consideration of the factors in s 25: *T v T (Financial Relief: Pensions)* (1998).

Section 31 of the MCA 1973: variation of orders

The court's powers are very wide in this area, but there are certain orders that cannot be varied. These are seen to be made in full and final settlement. They are:

- property adjustment orders;
- lump sum orders (unless ordered to be paid in instalments).

Usually, the need for a variation arises because of a change in circumstances of either the paying or receiving spouse. Examples are where the paying spouse has taken on the responsibilities of a second family; the receiving spouse has increased needs; or there has been an increase or decrease in the paying spouse's income. When considering applications for variation, the court shall have regard to all the circumstances of the case, including any changes in those circumstances, the first consideration being the welfare of a minor child of the family.

Also, in common with s 25A, the 'clean break' provision, the court has to decide whether to vary the order for a limited period under s 31(7). The court's attitude to both situations is similar, that is, it is often reluctant to apply a clean break. This reluctance to vary usually shows itself when a party applies for the termination of an order. The court has to consider whether or not the payee would be able to adjust to the new circumstances without undue hardship, and a major factor in its judgment would be any future uncertainty. The approach of the courts is often to refuse to terminate the order, instead reducing it to a nominal order so that, if the payee's circumstances were to deteriorate, he could apply for a further variation and the existence of the nominal order could be seen as a safeguard. It is also of note that the court can, on an application for variation, make a lump sum order or a property adjustment order, if they feel that this is the most appropriate way of dealing with the case, even though the variation request is in relation to a periodical payment order.

It should be remembered that, where the parties have agreed on the financial matters and consent orders have been made, the limitations regarding lump sums and property adjustment orders still apply; also, if a variation of a consent order is sought, then it will be necessary to show at least some of the following factors:

- fresh evidence coming to light which was not known at the time the order was made;
- the parties, including the court, relied on erroneous information;
- fraud or non-disclosure, the absence of which would have led to a substantially different order;
- exceptionally, the basis for the original order has been destroyed.

In order to avoid these hurdles, parties may appeal against an order out of time. However, there are strict limitations on this course of action and leave will only be granted if the applicant can meet the requirements laid down in *Barder v Barder* (1987). These requirements are that:

- new events invalidate the basis of the order and an appeal would be likely to succeed;
- the new event occurred within a few months of the order;
- the application is made reasonably promptly; and
- the appeal, if granted, would not prejudice third parties who had acted in good faith and for valuable consideration on the basis of the order.

The main reason for such a strict approach is to prevent numerous applications and to maintain certainty in those situations. Also, following *Piglowska v Piglowska* (1999), the House of Lords drew attention to the principle of proportionality between legal costs incurred and the assets available. It was felt that there had been too many hearings in this case and that, in future, consideration had to be given to such matters. Despite the warning on costs, it would appear that high costs are still being incurred in fighting ancillary relief cases. In *L v L* (2002), the wife's appeal against the original order was successful, but the Court of Appeal highlighted the fact that nearly £1 m had been spent by the parties in litigating.

Financial provision and property adjustment for children

The law is found in the Child Support Acts 1991 and 1995 (as amended by the Child Support, Pensions and Social Security Act 2000). Note that the following is based on the law as amended in 2000, which is finally due for implementation in March 2003. However, where children fall outside the limits, financial provision and property adjustment orders are available under the MCA 1973. The criteria are contained in s 25(3), which closely follows the criteria for adults.

Also, there is provision in s 15 and Sched 1 to the Children Act (CA) 1989 for financial relief for children. An application under the CA 1989 may be for periodical payments, lump sums, settlements and transfers of property (Sched 1 para 1). However, if the application is made in the Family Proceedings Court, only the monetary orders are available, not property orders.

The Child Support Acts

The Child Support Acts set out to establish a mechanism for the assessment and enforcement of child maintenance, but only in respect of periodical payments. The Acts do not cover other forms of child support. The functions to be carried out under the Acts are the responsibility of the Child Support Agency.

The Child Support Agency

This body was set up to deal with the maintenance of children by non-resident parents. Applications will be made to the Agency by the parent or person with care for the child for an order against the non-resident parent. Section 2 of the Child Support Act (CSA) 1991 states that the officers must have regard to the welfare of any child likely to be affected by decisions reached by use of their discretionary powers. However, the calculation of child support is subject to a strict straight line percentage deduction from income, and hence there is little scope for discretionary decisions.

To whom does the legislation apply?

The Acts only relate to those families falling within the definitions set out thus: there must be a qualifying child, a person with care and a non-resident parent.

Qualifying child ...

- Must have at least one non-resident parent
- Must be under 16 years of age or under 19 years if in FT education (not university) or specified training
- Must be resident in the UK

Non-resident parent ...

- Must be biological parent or adoptive parent
- Must not live in same household
- Must be resident in the UK

3 Ancillary Relief

```
         Person/parent
         with care ...
        /              \
Must live with the     Must be resident
child and provide      in the UK
day to day care
```

Using the Acts

Not all persons or parents with care are required to use the Agency and Acts as a means of child support calculation. Clearly, if the definitions are not applicable, there is no jurisdiction. If the Agency does have jurisdiction, then two scenarios apply:

Must use the Agency

- Qualifying child lives with a parent with care.
- Parent with care is receiving one of the specified welfare benefits (ie Income Support, income-related Job Seeker's Allowance, Disability Working Allowance) – the parent with care will be allowed to keep the first £10 of child support payable after assessment – the remainder 'pays back' the state for provision of welfare benefits for the child.

May use the Agency

- Qualifying child lives with a parent with care who is not claiming benefit.
- Qualifying child lives with person with care who may or may not be claiming benefit.

- Has a court order for child support (periodical payments) which was granted post 1993 and has been in existence for more than one year.

Failure to comply

If the parent with care falls into the first scenario and fails to comply with the Agency, the Agency will consider why this failure arises. If the parent with care can prove that compliance will result in violence or a threat of violence to themselves or the child, the Agency will treat non-compliance as justifiable. If the parent with care cannot prove this to the satisfaction of the Agency, the benefits payable to the parent with care will be reduced by up to 40%.

Assessing the child support payable

Only the non-resident parent (NRP) will be assessed in relation to their net income, and a variety of rates apply:

- a basic rate;
- a reduced rate;
- a flat rate; and
- a nil rate.

The basic rate is the following percentage of the NRP's net weekly income:

- 15% for one qualifying child;
- 20% for two qualifying children; and
- 25% for three or more qualifying children.

This will apply where the net weekly income is above £200, subject to a cap, whereby income over £2,000 per week will be ignored.

The reduced rate will apply when the net weekly income is below £200 but above £100 per week. Payments will be on a sliding scale according to the income level, but will not be less than £5 per week.

The flat rate of £5 per week is payable by NRPs whose net income is below £100 per week, who receive prescribed benefits, pensions or allowances, or whose partners receive prescribed benefits.

The nil rate applies if the NRP is of a prescribed description or has a weekly income of less than £5.

Where the NRP has a second, resident family, the net income will be calculated differently. The net income for the purposes of child support will be reduced by the relevant percentage applicable for the number of resident children – ie if there is one resident child, the net income for the purposes of child support is total net income less 15%.

Variations to child support

If the NRP has high costs relating to seeing the qualifying child, or in relation to employment, or has made a large capital transfer, pre 1993, to the parent with care with the intention of reducing child support, an application to reduce the basic amount payable can be made. These adjustments are known as departures, and in reality do not result in any major reduction in child support payable.

Enforcement of child support

The enforcement regime has been tightened up with regard to co-operation and payment of child support. Non-resident parents are now subject to a range of sanctions for non-compliance with the assessment process or payment:

- penalties of up to 25% for late/non-payment of support payments;
- deductions from earnings orders;

- liability orders for non-payment which may be enforced by distress;
- commitment to prison;
- disqualification from driving.

The court's role

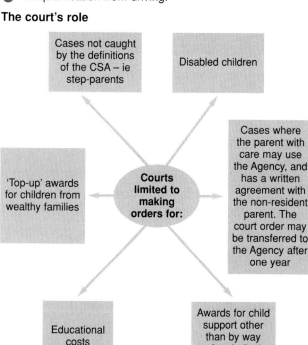

The legislation used to enable the court to make an order, and to assess what support is reasonable, will, depending on the status of the applicant and the respondent, be:

- the Matrimonial Causes Act 1973;
- the Domestic Proceedings and Magistrates' Courts Act 1978; or
- the Children Act 1989.

4 Family Homes and Domestic Violence

Part IV of the Family Law Act 1996

This deals with the reform of measures relating to the difficult area of domestic violence, which were previously contained in the Matrimonial Homes Act 1983, the Domestic Violence and Matrimonial Proceedings Act 1976 and the Domestic Proceedings and Magistrates' Courts Act 1978.

In *Richards v Richards* (1984), Scarman LJ described the situation as he saw it:

> The statutory provision is a hotchpotch of enactments of limited scope, passed into law to meet specific situations or to strengthen the powers of specified courts.

The aim of Part IV is to remove the complexity of the previous legislation, and to introduce a consistent range of remedies and criteria upon which they are based, throughout the courts that have jurisdiction in this area.

Rights to occupy matrimonial home (s 30)

Section 30(1) gives the non-estate holding spouse the right to occupy the matrimonial home if the other spouse is entitled to occupy by virtue of a beneficial estate or interest, a contract or any enactment.

These matrimonial home rights (MHRs) are:

- if in occupation, a right not to be evicted or excluded from the dwelling house or any part of it by the other spouse, except with the leave of the court given by a s 33 order;
- if not in occupation, a right (with the leave of the court) to enter into and occupy the dwelling house.

Section 31 states that MHRs are charges on the estate or interest of the other spouse and have the same priority as if an equitable interest has been created on one of the following dates, whichever is the latest:

- the date on which the spouse so entitled acquires the estate or interest;
- the date of the marriage; or
- 1 January 1968 (the commencement date of the Matrimonial Homes Act 1967).

Even though MHRs are charges, these rights are brought to an end by the death of the other spouse or upon termination of the marriage (other than by death), unless an order exists under s 33(5). The charge takes priority after an existing mortgage.

Occupation orders

Where a person is entitled to occupy a dwelling house by virtue of a beneficial estate, interest, contract or MHR in relation to a dwelling house, and that dwelling house is, has been or was intended to be the home of that person or another person associated with him, then he can apply for an occupation order. Where an agreement to marry is terminated, that person can also apply for such an order, but the application must be made within three years of the termination of the agreement. The time runs from the day that the agreement to marry ends.

The range of permitted applicants is narrower than for non-molestation orders and applicants are split into two categories – 'entitled' and 'non-entitled'. The concept of 'associated person' is not used. Section 62(1) defines cohabitants as 'a man and woman who, although not married to each other, are living together as husband and wife'. This would generally be seen to rule out applications by homosexual cohabitants; however, this view may have to change following the Court of Appeal's decision in *Mendoza v Ghaidan* (2002).

Occupation orders under s 33

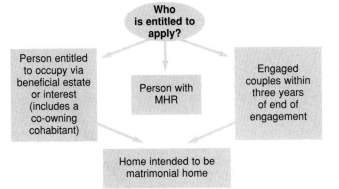

```
                    ┌─────────────────┐
                    │ Housing needs/  │
                    │ resources – the │
                    │  parties and any│
                    │ relevant children│
                    └─────────────────┘
                             ↑
┌──────────────┐      ┌─────────────┐      ┌──────────────┐
│  Financial   │      │ Criteria for│      │ Conduct of the│
│ resources of │ ←――→ │occupation order│ ←→│   parties in │
│ the parties  │      │  under s 33 │      │  relation to │
└──────────────┘      └─────────────┘      │  each other  │
                             ↓              │ and otherwise│
                    ┌─────────────────┐    └──────────────┘
                    │ Effect of making/│
                    │ refusing the order│
                    │  on grounds of   │
                    │  health, safety  │
                    │  or well being of│
                    │   parties and    │
                    │  relevant child  │
                    └─────────────────┘
                             ↓
                    ┌─────────────────────┐
                    │ 'Balance of harm' test applies:│
                    │  *Chalmers v Johns* (1999);    │
                    │  *B v B (Occupation Order)* (1999)│
                    └─────────────────────┘
```

Effect of the order

The order may:

- enforce the applicant's entitlement to remain in occupation as against the other person (the respondent);
- require the respondent to permit the applicant to enter and remain in the dwelling house or part of it;
- regulate the occupation of the dwelling house by either or both parties;
- if the respondent is entitled by virtue of a beneficial estate or interest or contract, prohibit, suspend or restrict the exercise of his right to occupy the dwelling house;
- if the respondent has MHRs in relation to the dwelling house and the applicant is the other spouse, restrict or terminate those rights;
- require the respondent to leave the dwelling house or part of it; or
- exclude the respondent from a defined area in which the dwelling house is included.

The important measure here is the power to exclude the respondent from a defined area.

Obligations that courts may apply to occupation orders

Orders under s 33

- Use of furniture and other contents
- Repair/rent/mortgages/other outgoings
- Periodical payments re accommodation

Duration of order

Under s 33, the court may make an order for a specified period (often quite short) or until a further order is made. If the applicant for the order is seeking it due to their MHRs (and hence the application is made during the subsistence of the marriage), the court can state that the order shall not end due to the death of the other party, or due to the termination of the marriage (otherwise than by death).

Occupation orders under ss 35, 36, 37 and 38

Occupation orders under these sections will refer to applicants within the specified status for each section. The criteria and effects of the orders are all similar to those for s 33 above, but with slight changes as highlighted below. The maximum duration of the order is specific to the individual section.

Section 35

- Applicant is a former spouse with no right to occupy the home
- Criteria – as for s 33, but with three extra factors
  - The length of time that has elapsed since the parties lived together
  - The length of time that has elapsed since the marriage was brought to an end
  - The existence of any pending proceedings relating to the property by way of an application for a property adjustment order, declaration of legal/beneficial ownership or an application under the CA 1989 for a property adjustment order.
- Duration – specified duration of up to six months with extension possible by application on one or more occasions for no longer than six months per application

Section 36

- Applicant is a cohabitant or former cohabitant with no existing right to occupy
- Criteria – as for s 33, but with six extra factors
  - The nature of the parties' relationship
  - The length of time that they have lived as husband and wife
  - Whether there are, or have been, any children of the parties or for whom they have/had parental responsibility
  - The length of time that has elapsed since the parties lived together
  - The existence of any pending proceedings relating to the property by way of a declaration of legal/beneficial ownership or an application under the CA 1989 for a property adjustment order.
  - The fact that the parties have not shown each other the commitment of marriage – this is linked to the first factor above (s 41)
- Duration – specified duration of up to six months with extension possible by application on one more occasion for no longer than six months

Section 37

- Applicant is a spouse or former spouse and neither party has a right to occupy
- Criteria – as for s 33
- Duration – specified duration of up to six months with extension possible by application on one or more occasions for no longer than six months per application

Section 38

- Applicant is a cohabitant or former cohabitant and neither party has a right to occupy

- Criteria – as s 33
- Duration – specified duration of up to six months with extension possible by application on one more occasion for no longer than six months

Transfer of tenancies

Another aspect of what arguably could be seen as protection, furthered by the Act in Sched 7, is the ability of the courts to transfer certain types of tenancies on divorce or separation of cohabitants.

The types of tenancies which are included are:

- a protected tenancy or statutory tenancy within the meaning of the Rent Act 1977;
- a statutory tenancy within the meaning of the Rent (Agriculture) Act 1976;
- a secure tenancy within the meaning of s 79 of the Housing Act 1985; and
- an assured tenancy or assured agricultural occupancy within the meaning of Part I of the Housing Act 1988.

The power is available to the court when one spouse is entitled to occupy a dwelling house by virtue of a relevant tenancy, either in his own right or jointly with the other spouse. The court also has power to make a property adjustment order under s 23A (divorce or separation) or s 24 (nullity). Where there is entitlement, it is also available to cohabitants who cease to live together as husband and wife.

The dwelling house in question must have been the matrimonial home of the spouses or the home where the cohabitants lived as husband and wife.

In deciding this matter, the court shall have regard to all the circumstances of the case, including:

- the circumstances in which the tenancy was granted to either or both parties or the circumstances in which they became tenants under the tenancy;
- the matters mentioned in s 36(6)(a)–(c) (needs and resources and considerations with respect to children) and, where the parties are cohabitants and only one of them is entitled to occupy the dwelling house by virtue of the relevant tenancy, the further matters mentioned in s 36(6)(e)–(h) (nature and length of relationship, children for whom they have had parental responsibility and how long they have lived apart); and
- the suitability of the parties as tenants. The court should also give the landlord of the dwelling house an opportunity to be heard.

Under s 53 and Part II of Sched 7, the court can transfer a tenancy from one party to the other or, if it is a joint tenancy, to one party alone. All the privileges, obligations, liabilities and any indemnities will be transferred along with the tenancy.

Under Part III, the court may order the transferee to pay compensation to the transferor, but may defer such payment or allow payment by instalments. When deciding these matters, the court will consider all the circumstances, as well as:

- the financial loss to the transferor that would otherwise occur as a result of the order;
- the financial needs and resources of the parties;
- the financial obligations that the parties have or are likely to have in the foreseeable future, including such obligations to each other and any children.

However, the ability to defer or allow instalments will only be available if to order immediate payment would cause the transferee greater financial hardship than that which would be suffered by the transferor if it was granted.

Even if the tenancy is transferred, the court may order that both parties should be jointly and severally liable for the discharge or performance of all obligations and liabilities in respect of the dwelling house which previously fell to only one of the parties. If such an order is made, the court may also direct that an indemnity by one party to the other be made for carrying out the obligations.

The appropriate time for transfers taking effect is, in the case of nullity, on the granting of the decree absolute and, in the case of divorce or separation, the date to be determined as if the court was making a property adjustment under s 23A of the Matrimonial Causes Act (MCA) 1973.

No application for a transfer can be made by a spouse after the remarriage of that spouse.

Non-molestation orders (s 42)

A non-molestation order is an order containing either or both of the following provisions:

- prohibiting a person (the respondent) from molesting another person who is associated with the respondent;
- prohibiting the respondent from molesting a relevant child.

The definitions of 'relevant child' and 'associated' are contained in s 62(2) and (3)–(5). The class of possible applicants for non-molestation orders has been significantly widened to provide greater protection in cases of domestic violence where the parties are not married and are not a heterosexual cohabiting couple. The following persons will be classed as associated:

- they are or have been married to one another;
- they are or have been cohabitants (meaning a heterosexual cohabiting couple living as if man and wife);

- they live in the same household other than by virtue of being an employee, tenant, lodger or boarder (this would hence cover same-sex relationships);
- they are relatives;
- they are engaged to be married, or have been engaged (subject to a three year limit after termination of the engagement);
- in relation to a child they are parents, or have/had parental responsibility;
- they are parties to family proceedings, other than under Part IV of the Family Law (FLA) 1996.

Applications

The court can make a non-molestation order:

- on an application made by a person associated with the respondent (with or without other family proceedings); or
- if, in any family proceedings to which the respondent is a party, the court considers that the order should be made for the benefit of the other party to the proceedings or any

relevant child, even though no application has been made.

A child under the age of 16 cannot make an application for a non-molestation order without the leave of the court. The court may grant leave only if it considers that the child has sufficient understanding to make the application for a non-molestation order.

'Family proceedings' are defined as proceedings under the inherent jurisdiction of the High Court in relation to children and the following enactments:

- Parts II and IV of the FLA 1996;
- the MCA 1973;
- the Adoption Act 1976;
- the Domestic Proceedings and Magistrates' Courts Act 1978;
- Part III of the Matrimonial and Family Proceedings Act 1984;
- Parts I, II and IV of the Children Act 1989;
- s 30 of the Human Fertilisation and Embryology Act 1990; and
- s 44A of the Children Act 1989.

What is molestation?

A non-molestation order can be made to cover either particular or general molestation and can be made for a specified period or until further order. Examples of behaviour considered to be molestation can be seen in the following cases:

- *Horner v Horner* (1982): the husband handed the wife upsetting notes and intercepted her on her way to the station.
- *Johnson v Walton* (1990): the husband sent embarrassing photographs of his wife to a local

newspaper with intent to cause her distress. The court said that molestation can include *any* behaviour intended to cause distress or harm.

If the order is made within family proceedings, it will cease to have effect when those proceedings are withdrawn or dismissed. Non-molestation orders, traditionally, were not granted for a lengthy period, being seen as first aid rather than major surgery. The FLA simply states that the order may be made 'until further order', leaving the duration to the discretion of the court (*M v W (Non-Molestation Order: Duration)* (2000)). Orders may be varied or discharged by the court by application of the original applicant, or the respondent. In addition the court can vary or discharge the order on its own motion.

Criteria for granting non-molestation orders

All circumstances of case, including need to secure health, safety and well being of ...

- Applicant or person for whose benefit order is made
- Relevant child

As the need for protection from violence can arise in emergencies, there may be a need for orders without notice, and the court has the power under s 45 to grant such orders. Non-molestation orders can be granted without notice to the respondent if the court considers that it is just and convenient to do so. (This power is also available for occupation orders but very rarely used in this situation.)

When deciding these matters, the court will consider all the circumstances, including:

- any risk of significant harm to the applicant or a relevant child attributable to the conduct of the respondent if an order is not made immediately; and
- whether it is likely that the applicant will be deterred or prevented from pursuing the application if an order is not made immediately; and
- whether there is reason to believe that the respondent is aware of the proceedings but is deliberately evading service and the applicant or a relevant child will be seriously prejudiced by the delay involved:
  - where the court is a magistrates' court, in effecting service of proceedings; or
  - in any other case, in effecting substituted service.

The court must allow the respondent an opportunity to make representations at a full hearing as soon as it is just and convenient to do so. If the court makes an occupation order at the full hearing, then, as regards the period of six months, the time will run from the making of the initial order, as will the provisions regarding extensions.

Powers of arrest

Available if respondent has used/threatened to use violence against applicant/relevant child	Power attached unless adequate protection without the power

If no power of arrest attached and applicant considers that respondent has failed to comply with order, applicant can seek warrant

Under s 47, the court, on making an occupation order or a non-molestation order, where it appears that the respondent has used or threatened violence against the applicant or relevant child, shall attach a power of arrest to one or more of the provisions of the order unless it is satisfied that the applicant or child will be adequately protected without such a power. Thus, there is a presumption that there will be a power of arrest attached.

This does not apply to orders without notice, but the court can attach a power of arrest if it is satisfied that the respondent has used or threatened violence against the applicant or relevant child and there is a risk of significant harm to the applicant or relevant child, attributable to the conduct of the respondent, if the power of arrest is not attached to the provisions immediately.

If the power of arrest is attached, then a constable may arrest without warrant a person whom he has reasonable cause for suspecting to be in breach of any such provision. A person who is arrested must be brought before the relevant judicial authority within 24 hours and, if the matter is not disposed of then, he may be remanded.

If the court has made an order but has not attached a power of arrest or has only attached the power to certain provisions of the order, then, if the applicant considers that the respondent has failed to comply with the order, he may apply to the court for the issue of a warrant for the arrest of the respondent. The court may only issue the warrant if it is satisfied that the application is substantiated on oath and has reasonable grounds for believing that the respondent has failed to comply with the order.

Undertakings

In any case where the court can make occupation orders or non-molestation orders, the court may accept an undertaking from any party to the proceedings and no power of arrest can be attached to an undertaking. However, the court shall not accept an undertaking in any case where, apart from this restriction, a power of arrest would be attached.

Amendments to the Children Act 1989

Important additions to the protective powers available to the courts have been introduced by amendments to Sched 6 to the Children Act.

Under s 38A of the Children Act, where the court is satisfied that the requirements for an interim care order have been met, the court may include an exclusion requirement if:

(a) there is reasonable cause to believe that, if a person (the relevant person) is excluded from a dwelling house in which the child lives, the child will cease to suffer or cease to be likely to suffer significant harm; and
(b) another person living in the dwelling house (whether a parent of the child or some other person):
    (i) is able and willing to give to the child the care which it would be reasonable to expect a parent to give him; and
    (ii) consents to the inclusion of the exclusion requirement.

The court has the power to attach the power of arrest to an exclusion requirement. A constable may arrest without warrant any person whom he has reasonable cause to believe to be in breach of the requirement.

If, while the interim care order with an exclusion requirement is in force, the local authority removes the child from the dwelling house from which the relevant person is excluded for a continuous period of more than 24 hours, the exclusion requirement of the order will cease to have effect. If the court accepts an undertaking in place of making an exclusion requirement, then no power of arrest can be attached.

Under s 44A of the Children Act 1989, the court now also has the ability to attach an exclusion requirement to an emergency protection order if it is satisfied that:

(a) there is reasonable cause to believe that if a person (the relevant person) is excluded from a dwelling house in which the child lives, then:
   (i) in the case of an order made on the ground mentioned in s 44(1)(a), the child will not be likely to suffer significant harm, even though the child is not removed as mentioned in s 44(1)(a)(i) or does not remain as mentioned in s 44(1)(a)(ii); or
   (ii) in the case of an order made on the ground mentioned in para (b) or (c) of s 44(1), the inquiries referred to in that paragraph will cease to be frustrated; and
(b) another person living in the dwelling house (whether a parent of the child or some other person):
   (i) is able and willing to give to the child the care which it would be reasonable to expect a parent to give him; and
   (ii) consents to the inclusion of the exclusion requirement.

The factors to be considered when dealing with the power of arrest are the same as the case with the interim care order, as is the situation with undertakings. Also, the definition of an exclusion requirement is common to both sections:

(a) a provision requiring the relevant person to leave a dwelling house in which he is living with the child;
(b) a provision prohibiting the relevant person from entering a dwelling house in which the child lives;

(c) a provision excluding the relevant person from a defined area in which the dwelling house in which the child lives is situated.

```
                    Exclusion requirement
                         added to
                    ↙              ↘
       Interim care              Emergency protection
       order – s 38A             order – s 44A
```

Both end if local authority removes child from dwelling house from where respondent is excluded for a continuous period of over 24 hours

Power of arrest factors apply

Protection from Harassment Act 1997

Although Part IV of the FLA 1996 has increased the amount of protection available in cases of domestic violence for family members and other 'associated persons', there is still a need to protect those not covered by the FLA.

The main provisions of the Act are as follows.

Section 1(1)

A person must not pursue a course of conduct:

(a) which amounts to harassment of another; and

(b) which he knows or ought to know amounts to harassment of another.

- 'Course of conduct' – at least two occasions s 7(3).
- 'Harassment' – includes speech: s 7(4).
- 'Knows/ought to know' – objective test: s 1(2).

Section 1(3) contains exemptions if the person pursuing the conduct can show that:

- it was pursued for the purpose of preventing/detecting crime;
- it was pursued under any enactment or rule of law or to comply with any condition or requirement imposed by any person under any enactment; or
- in the particular circumstances, the pursuit of the course of conduct was reasonable.

The purpose of these exemptions is to allow certain occupations to be followed without the persons involved committing an offence, for example, investigative journalists, debt collectors, private investigators, etc. It is up to the persons claiming exemption to show that it applies.

Criminal offences

Section 2

A person who breaches s 1 is guilty of harassment.

Summary conviction . . . . six months and/or fine.

Section 4

Putting people in fear of violence.
  Section 4(1): course of conduct – at least two occasions – causes another to fear violence if he knows/ought to know that the conduct will cause the other to fear violence on those occasions. Again, an objective test: s 4(2).

Section 4(3) contains exemptions, as in s 1(3) above.

Summary conviction . . . . six months and/or fine.
Conviction on indictment . . . . five years and/or fine.

If the defendant is found not guilty of a s 4 offence, he may still be found guilty of a s 2 offence.

Section 5

Allows a court to impose a restraining order on a person convicted of a s 4 offence. The order will last for a specified period or until further order.

The order will prohibit:

- further harassment;
- putting people in fear of violence.

Breach of such an order:

Summary conviction . . . . six months and/or fine.
Conviction on indictment . . . . five years and/or fine.

Civil remedies

Section 3

Section 3(1): allows a civil claim for an actual or apprehended breach of s 1 by the victim of the course of conduct.

Section 3(2): court may award damages for, for example, anxiety caused by the harassment and any financial loss resulting from the harassment.

Section 3(3): the High Court/county court may grant injunctions restraining the defendant from pursuing harassing conduct, and, if the claimant considers that there has been a breach, he may apply for a warrant for the arrest of the defendant.

5 Children I

The nature of the relationship between parents and their children, and the respective rights that they hold, is subject to change as societal views alter. Today there is an increasing recognition of children's individual rights, and the fact that these exist in parallel with, or to the exclusion of, parental rights. However, a child may not always be in a position to exercise rights, perhaps due to their age, and so the law places duties on parents to do so. The state of flux that exists between the extent of parents' rights vis à vis children's rights is illustrated in the case of *Gillick v West Norfolk AHA* (1986). This case introduced the concept of the *Gillick* competent child, one who was of sufficient age and understanding to take decisions for themselves, rather than this resting with the parents. Although the extent of *Gillick* in terms of reducing the role for parents may be overstated, the case has informed the major piece of legislation relating to children, the Children Act 1989. This Act does not set out in detail the nature of parents' duties in relation to their children, these being established in case law.

```
Discipline  ←—  General parental duties  —→  Education
    ↓
If                Physical                Maintenance
reasonable         care
                    ↓                        ↓
               Indicates                 In money
           medical treatment/          or money's worth
            protection from
              abuse/harm
```

The Children Act 1989

The Children Act 1989 introduced a variety of new principles into the operation of the law in family relationships. It emphasises the importance of the child's welfare, how the child's needs should be met, the extent to which the state (whether the court or a local authority) can intervene, and establishes key concepts, such as parental responsibility.

An important aim of the Act is to provide a flexible, consistent set of remedies and orders which will be available at all levels of the legal system and to make them available whether the matter is one of private or public law. This attempt at unification of both areas of law has been largely successful and has provided much of the sought-after flexibility.

5 Children I

Parental responsibility

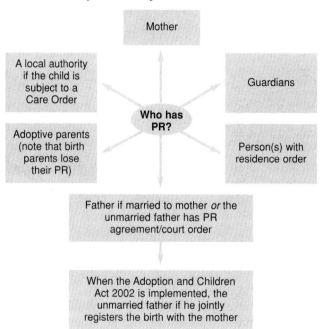

Person(s) with PR can act independently of others, except:

- if consent is required from all with PR;
- if this would be in contravention of a court order; or
- if PR is held as a result of a care order.

Parental responsibility cannot be given away. The parents will retain it even if they divorce. If the child is made the subject of a care order, they will share it with the local authority, and they cannot transfer it to another party in an attempt to avoid their responsibilities. PR can be brought to an end by the child being adopted, resulting in the PR being vested in the adoptive parents, and on the child reaching maturity, marrying or joining the armed forces.

Guardians

The position relating to guardians is now much more restricted than prior to the implementation of the Children Act 1989, and the only methods of making an appointment are contained in s 5 of the Act.

Section 5(1) gives the court the power to appoint an individual who applies to be a guardian in respect of a child if:

- the child has no parent with parental responsibility for him; or
- a residence order has been made in respect of the child in favour of a parent or guardian who died while the order was in force.

Section 5(3) allows a parent with parental responsibility to appoint an individual to be his child's guardian in the event of that parent's death. The appointment should be made in writing, and must be dated and witnessed by two witnesses.

The appointment will only take effect if:

- on the death of the parent making the appointment, there is no other parent with parental responsibility for the child; or
- immediately before the death of the parent making the appointment, a residence order in that parent's favour was in force with respect to the child (s 5(7)).

If there is no residence order, the surviving parent retains PR and the guardian's appointment only takes effect when that person has also died (s 5(8)). On appointment, the guardian has PR for the child (s 5(6)).

The revocation and disclaimer of an appointment

Section 6 states that a later appointment by a parent or guardian will be taken to revoke the earlier appointment unless it is clear (either by express provision or necessary implication) that the purpose of the later appointment is to make an additional appointment.

It also allows the parent to revoke the appointment by another written document which meets the requirements needed for an appointment or by destroying the original document. If the appointment is made by will, then this must be revoked.

If a person has been appointed as a child's guardian but wishes to disclaim his appointment, he can do so by an instrument in writing and signed by him, which must be made within a reasonable time of his first knowing that the appointment has taken effect. The obvious way to avoid difficulties would be to consult with the person to be appointed prior to making the arrangements, thus making a disclaimer unnecessary.

The court has the power to bring an appointment of a guardian to an end on the application of any person with PR, on the application of the child concerned with leave of the court and in any family proceedings, if the court considers that it should be brought to an end even though no application has been made.

When dealing with matters of guardianship, the court should apply the principles contained in s 1(1), (2) and (5).

Although it need not do so, it will normally also apply the checklist in s 1(3) (see below).

Key principles in s 1

s 1(1) — The child's welfare is the court's paramount concern when dealing with issues relating to the child's upbringing or the child's property. Does not apply to financial provisions for child support/maintenance, Adoption Act 1976 applications (note changes in Adoption and Children Act 2002), applications for leave (see later).

s 1(2) — Delay to be avoided in progressing cases, as deemed prejudicial to child's welfare. Planned, purposeful delay acceptable (*C v Solihull MBC* (1993)).

s 1(3) & 1(4) — Sets out the so called 'welfare checklist'. A list of factors for the courts to assess what is in the welfare of the child, in the situations indicated by sub-s (4).

s 1(5) — The no-order principle. The court should not make an order under the CA 1989 unless they consider that making the order would be better for the child than making no order at all: *B v B (A Minor: Grandparents: Residence Order)* (1992).

The welfare checklist

Section 1(3) contains what has become commonly known as the 'checklist' – the factors that the court is required to consider when dealing with the circumstances mentioned in s 1(4).

These situations are:

- where the court is being asked to make, vary or discharge a s 8 order and this is disputed by one of the parties;
- where the court is considering whether to make, vary or discharge an order under Part IV (see later).

Whilst in other situations the court is not required to refer to the checklist, in reality this is frequently done.

The factors which the court considers are:

- the ascertainable wishes and feelings of the child concerned (considered in the light of his age and understanding);
- the likely effect on him of any change in his circumstances;
- his physical, emotional and educational needs;
- his age, sex, background and any characteristic of his which the court considers relevant;
- any harm which he has suffered or is at risk of suffering;
- how capable each of his parents and any other person in relation to whom the court considers the question to be relevant is of meeting his needs;
- the range of powers available to the court under the Act in the proceedings in question.

What sort of things does the court look at?

The ascertainable wishes and feelings of the child

This factor develops the philosophy of '*Gillick* competence'. The child's wishes will be judged in the light of his age and understanding.

The likely effect on the child of any change in his circumstances

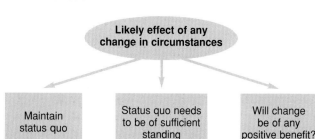

The child's physical, emotional and educational needs

- Physical care, including housing
- Well being not dependent on material matters alone
- Continuity of care by one person (*not* babysitters)
- **Physical, emotional and educational needs**
- No automatic order in favour of mother – consideration *not* presumption
- Education
- Siblings

The child's age, sex, background and any characteristics which the court considers relevant

Sex, background, relevant characteristics

- Boys with fathers, girls with mothers
- Cultural/ethnic/religious background

Starting point, but where a dispute exists, only a consideration, not a presumption: *Re S (A Minor) (Custody)* (1991).
Courts often link to maintaining the status quo, and reflect the decision reached by the parties themselves

Any harm which the child has suffered or is at risk of suffering

Harm

- Important duty to prevent any harm
- New partners of parents with care
- Allegations of sexual abuse – standard of proof: *Re H & Others* (1996)
- Parents' sexual preferences

  Lesbian mothers/Homosexual fathers

  This is increasingly outdated, and unless proven to be harmful, potentially discriminatory

  Aim for situation nearest to ideal or the best available

5 Children I

The capability of each parent to meet the child's needs

Capability of each parent
- Evidence of capability via care, resources
- Allowing child to achieve full potential

The range of powers available to the court under this Act in the proceedings in question

Range of powers
- Section 8 orders
- Family assistance orders
- Part V orders
- Interim care order
- Sections 7, 37, 47 inquiries
- Section 1 principles apply when required but also often applied as 'good practice'
- Orders under Part IV – care or supervision orders

Private law orders

These are the orders that the court is most likely to be asked to grant in proceedings between two individuals – that is, divorcing spouses. However, it is not unusual for a private law order to be made in proceedings commenced by the local authority, since the court must consider the full range of options available to it.

Section 8 orders

The orders are:

- residence orders;
- contact orders;
- prohibited steps orders; and
- specific issues orders.

Section 10(1) of the Act gives the court the power to make s 8 orders in any family proceedings in which a question arises with respect to the welfare of any child if:

- an application for the order has been made by a person who:
  - is entitled to apply for a s 8 order with respect to the child; or
  - has obtained the leave of the court to make the application; or
- the court considers that the order should be made even though no such application has been made.

The first point of note is 'What are family proceedings?'. The definition is contained in s 8(3) and (4).

Section 8(3)

For the purposes of this Act, 'family proceedings' means any proceedings:

(a) under the inherent jurisdiction of the High Court in relation to children; and
(b) under the enactments mentioned in sub-s (4), but does not include proceedings on an application for leave under s 100(3).

Section 8(4)

The enactments are:

(a) Parts I, II and IV of this Act;
(b) the MCA 1973;
(c) the Adoption Act 1976;
(d) the Domestic Proceedings and Magistrates' Courts Act 1978;
(e) Part III of the Matrimonial and Family Proceedings Act 1984;
(f) the Family Law Act 1996
(g) the Human Fertilisation and Embryology Act 1990;
(h) ss 11 and 12 of the Crime and Disorder Act 1998.

Who can apply for s 8 orders?

Section 10(4)

The following persons are entitled to apply to the court for any s 8 order with respect to a child:

(a) any parent or guardian of the child;
(b) any person in whose favour a residence order is in force with respect to the child.

Section 10(5)

The following persons are entitled to apply for a residence or contact order with respect to the child:

(a) any party to a marriage (whether or not subsisting), in relation to whom the child is a child of the family;
(b) any person with whom the child has lived for a period of at least three years;
(c) any person who:
   (i) in any case where a residence order is in force with respect to the child, has the consent of each of the persons in whose favour the order was made;
   (ii) in any case where the child is in the care of the local authority, has the consent of that authority;
   (iii) in any other case, has the consent of each of those (if any) who have parental responsibility for the child.

An example of the flexibility brought into the area of remedies available under the Children Act 1989 is the fact that any person can apply for a s 8 order. If they are not included in the above groups, then they must apply to the court for leave to apply for an order (s 10(1)(a)(ii)).

The factors that the court has to consider when dealing with an application for leave are contained in s 10(9):

(a) the nature of the proposed application for the s 8 order;
(b) the applicant's connection with the child;
(c) any risk of that proposed application disrupting the child's life to such an extent that he would be harmed by it; and
(d) where the child is being looked after by a local authority:
   (i) the authority's plans for the child's future; and
   (ii) the wishes and feelings of the child's parents.

Foster parents

A problem could arise under s 9(3) in cases where the child has been in foster care. Where the child is, or has been at any time within the last six months, in foster care, then the person who had care of the child (that is, the foster parent) may not apply for leave to apply for a s 8 order unless:

- he has the consent of the authority;
- he is a relative of the child; or
- the child has lived with him for at least three years preceding the application.

The time period mentioned in this restriction need not be continuous, but must have begun not more than five years before the making of the application.

Welfare principle in leave applications

```
                    Child's welfare
                   /              \
    Is *not* paramount        *Is* paramount during
    during leave application   the full hearing
```

When can children apply for s 8 orders?

A child needing advice may well be able to help himself by applying for a s 8 order.

He must apply for leave to apply for such an order, and the court, in order to grant leave, must be satisfied that the child has sufficient understanding to make the proposed application. This will obviously be judged on the age and maturity of the particular child involved in each case. Because of the difficulties which arise in these cases, such applications should be heard by the High Court (*Practice Direction (Application by Children: Leave)* (1993)).

Child applications for leave

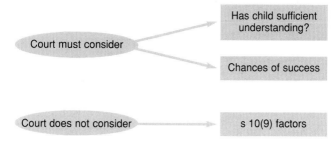

Restrictions on making s 8 orders

The court is limited in relation to section 8 orders in that they cannot be made in all situations:

s 9(6): court should not make a s 8 order to have effect after child has reached the age of 16 unless satisfied that the circumstances of the case are exceptional;

s 9(7): court should not make a s 8 order, other than varying or discharging such an order, with respect to a child who has reached the age of 16, unless satisfied that the circumstances of the case are exceptional.

Residence and contact orders are considered to be the primary orders in s 8 of the Act. Prohibited steps orders and specific issues orders are seen as secondary orders, as illustrated by the restrictions placed on their use by s 9(5).

By virtue of this sub-section, the court cannot exercise its power to make either order with a view to achieving a result which could be achieved by making a residence or contact order, or in any way which is denied to the High Court (by s 100(2)) in the exercise of its inherent jurisdiction with respect to children. It is said that it prevents the use of such orders in order to achieve certain aims via 'the back door' and ensures that the primary orders and inherent jurisdiction are used in the appropriate circumstances.

In *Nottinghamshire CC v P* (1993), it was held that a prohibited steps order which prevented contact between the father and the children and excluded the father from the family home could not be allowed to stand, as it was seen as achieving a result which could be achieved by the making of a residence or contact order, and the local authority was attempting to use the 'back door' approach to the problem.

Residence orders

Residence orders (ROs) settle the arrangements to be made as to the person with whom the child is to live.

The necessity for an RO most frequently occurs in family breakdown situations and is used to settle disputes over what was previously known as custody. The intention behind the order is not just to decide who has possession of the child; it will also mean that they take on the everyday responsibilities of care for the child. Because of this, the matter of parental responsibility must be considered – in order to fulfil this task, the person with the RO must be able to take everyday decisions regarding the upbringing of the child. If an RO is granted to a married parent, then it will not alter the situation that each parent will retain parental responsibility and each is able to act independently for the benefit of the child. If the order is granted to an unmarried father, the court is obliged to grant him parental responsibility by way of a s 4 'parental responsibility order' (s 12(1)), which he will share with the mother.

If the order is granted to a non-parent, they will be granted shared parental responsibility with the parent (s 12(2)), but it will be limited, in as much as the non-parent will be unable to consent to or refuse to consent to an adoption or appoint a guardian (s 12(3)).

Limits on residence orders

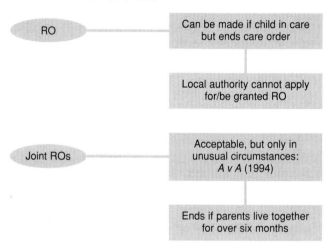

Following the granting of a residence order, s 13 of the Act must be considered. It states that, if such an order is in force, no person may:

- cause the child to be known by a new surname; or
- remove him from the UK for over one month,

without the written consent of every person who has parental responsibility for the child or the leave of the court.

With regard to changing the child's surname, the court must be involved not only if there is an RO in existence, but also where any parent, with or without PR, objects to the change. The child's best interests will be of prime importance together with the reasons for seeking the change (*Dawson v Wearmouth* (1999)). If the child is old enough, their views will be taken into account. The courts are increasingly taking a very pragmatic approach in these cases (*Re R (A Child)* (2001)).

Again, when considering whether to grant leave for the child to leave the country, the court must bear in mind s 1, that is, the welfare and 'no order' principles. The cases which occur in this area often concern a family wishing to emigrate with the child.

Contact orders

This is an order requiring the person with whom the child lives, or is to live, to allow the child to visit or to stay with the person named in the order, or for the named person and the child otherwise to have contact with each other.

The order covers the area formerly known as access. It allows the non-resident parent or any other person named in the order to retain contact with the child, in a way to be decided by the court. This could be by stays, visits, letters or telephone calls, depending on the circumstances of the case.

M v M (1973)

Traditional view
Contact with parents is the right of the child, not of the parents.

Post-Human Rights Act 1998
Contact is a right of both the child and the parents and the court's role is to establish whose right is greater (*Hendricks v Netherlands* (1983); *B v UK* (1988)).

Court's attitude to contact

When reaching its decision on the matter of contact, the court must bear in mind that the paramount consideration is the welfare of the child. If there is conflict between the parties, the s 1(3) checklist must also be borne in mind. This is frequently the case, as these orders are usually sought in cases of family breakdown – bitterness and resentment can lead to a failure to reach an amicable agreement.

The accepted approach to the subject of contact is that there is a presumption that the child will be benefited by retaining contact with both parents, and contact should be allowed unless it can be shown to be detrimental to the child's welfare, as was illustrated in *Re H (Minors) (Access)* (1992). If there is a contested application for contact, then it is a matter for the court to decide on s 1 considerations.

Of particular concern is the question of domestic violence, primarily where the child is not a victim but may have observed violence, or the caring parent is at risk. It had been suggested that the courts were ignoring or reducing the impact of violence, or fears of it, and ordering contact due to the presumption of automatic benefit. Following the publication of *Making Contact Work* (Consultation Paper

(2001)) and the *Final Report* (2002), together with the decision in *Re L, Re V, Re M, Re H* (2000), the courts are more reluctant to order contact where domestic violence is an issue without first considering the evidence very carefully.

Under usual circumstances, it will be seen that a contact order will be granted to allow contact between the child and a non-resident parent, but the problem has arisen of whether a contact order can be made ordering that there be no contact between them. However, it is now clear that a contact order under s 8 can include an order for 'no-contact' (*Nottinghamshire CC v P (No 2)* (1993)).

Section 11(7) allows the court to attach directions as to how s 8 orders are to be carried out and to attach conditions: *Re O (Contact: Imposition of Conditions)* (1995). In this case, indirect contact was ordered and a condition was imposed that the mother should allow letters to be sent to the child and allow presents sent by the father to be opened. She was also to send photographs of the child and information relating to school reports, etc, to the father.

Enforcement of contact

The enforcement of contact orders are problematic in a variety of ways, from the caring parent not handing the child over, to the person entitled to contact not taking it up. With regard to the former, the courts have a variety of options, from altering the order to try to get something that is workable, through to changing the RO, or ultimately committing the non-co-operative parent to prison – *A v N (Committal: Refusal of Contact)* (1997). With the latter, it is much harder to establish a mechanism whereby the non-resident parent can be forced to attend for contact, and statistics show a dramatic reduction in the numbers of fathers who maintain contact after a period of two years. As contact is a right of the child, and given the State's responsibility to protect individuals' rights under the

European Convention on Human Rights, some method of enforcement should be considered. This has been noted in the *Making Contact Work* documents referred to above.

Supervised contact

> If contact needs to be supervised, for example, sexual abuse cases where contact is to continue

> Best practice is to use a s 16 family assistance order:
> *Re DH (A Minor) (Child Abuse)* (1994)
> *Re L (Contact: Transsexual Applicant)* (1995)

All the parties named in a s 16 family assistance order (FAO), with the exception of the child, must consent to the order being made. The maximum duration of an FAO is six months, which can limit the utility of the order in these circumstances.

Prohibited steps orders

These are defined in the Act as:

> ... an order that no step which could be taken by a parent in meeting his parental responsibility for a child and which is of the kind specified in the order.

It will be seen that the order covers steps which fall within the area of parental responsibility. As such, it is to some extent limited in its application, in as much as it cannot be used to prevent steps which would not come within this ambit, for example, assault or molestation; other measures would be needed in those circumstances.

This type of order is intended to deal with individual or single issues in a particular case, and is meant to prevent a particular step being taken. A common example would be an order preventing the removal of a child from the UK in a case where there was no residence order in force, and so no prohibition under s 13 to prevent such removal.

Normally, such an order would be made against one of the parents of the child who can, as we have seen, exercise his responsibility alone, provided that it is not incompatible with a court order. However, this order can be made against 'any person'. A person who could be named in the order may be any person that could take a step via parental responsibility. This might include a teacher or an unmarried father who does not have parental responsibility and could be prevented from consenting to medical treatment for the child.

Specific issues order

This is defined as:

> ... an order giving a direction for the purpose of determining a specific question which has arisen or which may arise in connection with any aspect of parental responsibility for a child.

Again, it will be seen that it is normally intended to deal with a single issue, and so is similar to a prohibited steps order. It is also limited by the requirement that the matter be within the area of parental responsibility. Where there is a dispute between the parents on a specific matter, the court can resolve the matter by granting this type of order and stating the necessary course of action. Such an area of conflict could be the issue of a child's education, as was the case in *Re P (A Minor) (Education: Child's Views)* (1992).

Another important case involving the granting of a specific issues order was *Re HG (Specific Issue: Sterilisation)* (1993), where it was held that, as there was an element of parental responsibility present in deciding the question of the child's treatment, the availability of a specific issue order was beyond question. The procedure for deciding such questions was also laid down for use in future cases. Other less draconian medical matters can be dealt with using a specific issues order, as in, for example, *Re J (Specific Issue Orders: Child's Religious Upbringing and Circumcision)* (2000).

Family assistance order

A new type of order introduced by the Children Act 1989 is the FAO, contained in s 16 of the Act.

In family proceedings, the court can make an FAO requiring either a probation officer or a local authority officer, usually a social worker, to be made available to advise, assist and befriend any person named in the order. However, before the order can be made, the local authority must agree to making the officer available (s 16(7)).

The persons that can be named in the order are those mentioned in s 16(2). They are:

- the child himself;
- the parent or guardian of the child;
- any person with whom the child is living or who has a contact order in his favour in respect of the child.

With the exception of the child, these persons, when named in the order, are also required to consent to the order being made (s 16(3)). The order can only be made for a maximum of six months and will only be available in exceptional circumstances.

This order will only be made by the court on its own motion and no applications can be made for this type of order. Due to the short time scale and the difficulties in getting a social worker appointed, whilst the making of the order may be seen as best practice, in reality they are little used.

6 Children II

Social service investigations

A local authority social services department (LA) has a range of obligations under the Children Act (CA) 1989, to assist and provide services to children in need, and to ensure that children are protected from abusive situations wherever possible. In order to enable the LA to decide what steps, if any, to take in relation to a child, the CA 1989 gives them a power of investigation under s 47. The duty to investigate a child's situation arises if:

- the child is subject to an emergency protection order (EPO) granted in favour of an applicant other than the LA;
- the child is subject to police protection under s 46;
- the LA has reasonable cause to suspect that the child is suffering or is likely to suffer significant harm.

The purpose of the investigation will be to:

- see if the LA should apply for an order under the CA 1989 to safeguard and protect the child;
- see if a child subject to an EPO, who is not being provided with local authority accommodation, should be so provided;
- see if a child subject to police protection should be made subject to an EPO.

To carry out an effective investigation the LA should see the family and seek evidence of significant harm, and establish what action is needed to prevent the child suffering significant harm.

Short term orders

Child assessment orders

Requirements

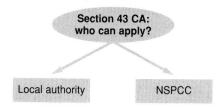

Grounds (s 43(1)):

- the applicant has reasonable cause to suspect that the child is suffering/likely to suffer significant harm;
- an assessment of the state of the child's health or development or of the way in which he has been treated is required to enable the applicant to determine whether or not the child is suffering or is likely to suffer significant harm; and
- it is unlikely that such an assessment will be made or be satisfactory in the absence of an order under this section.

The court, being the Family Proceedings Court, will base its decision on the child's welfare and the order will require the parents or carers to produce the child for assessment or allow the child to be visited in order for an assessment to be carried out. This means that the child can remain with the family whilst any assessment is carried out. If the child has to go elsewhere for assessment, for example, a hospital, and has to stay away from home for a few days, then the court can give directions as to contact and may specify the length of time he can be kept there.

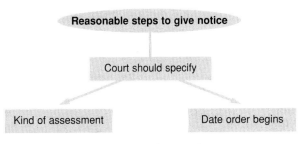

Duration: seven days maximum

The order should also specify how to make the assessment, but a child of sufficient understanding can refuse to undergo any form of assessment contained in the order (s 43(8)).

If the parents refuse to comply with the assessment order, there appears to be no direct form of enforcement. However, the local authority could inform them that, if they continue to fail to comply with the order, it could lead to the authority making an application for an EPO.

An important point to bear in mind when considering an assessment order is that, if the court thinks that grounds exist for the granting of an EPO, it may treat the application as an application for an emergency protection order and grant the order if the grounds are shown to exist (s 43(4)). There are problems with this sort of order, as it focuses on assessment and does not really have a protective element – it is more of an evidence gathering order. The order is used very infrequently and would seem to be utilised more as a threat to gain parents' co-operation in an investigation.

Emergency protection orders (EPOs)

These are short term protective orders which permit the applicant (normally the LA) to remove the child to a safe environment. There are three different criteria that can be used to gain an order, and as with the CAO, applications will be made to the Family Proceedings Court:

s 44(1)(a)	Applicant Criteria	Any person (includes LA). There is reasonable cause to believe that the child is likely to suffer significant harm if he is not removed to accommodation provided by the applicant or he does not remain where he is currently accommodated.
s 44(1)(b)	Applicant Criteria	LA. LA is carrying out a s 47 investigation. The enquiries are being frustrated by access being denied. Access is needed as a matter of urgency.
s 44(1)(c)	Applicant Criteria	NSPCC. The applicant has reasonable cause to suspect that the child is suffering or is likely to suffer significant harm. The applicant is making enquiries. The enquiries are being frustrated by access being denied. Access is needed as a matter of urgency.

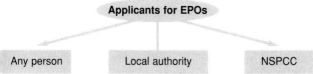

Application made to Family Proceedings Court

Duration: up to eight days and one extension only of up to seven days

| *Ex parte* applications possible to single justice | Notification to parents within 48 hours |

The effects of an emergency protection order

Section 44(4) allows the court to direct any person who is in a position to do so to produce the child to the applicant and authorises their removal to, or retention in, accommodation provided by the applicant, or prevent the removal of the child from some other place where he was being accommodated immediately prior to the order.

It is an offence to prevent the removal of the child or to obstruct a person exercising the power to remove the child.

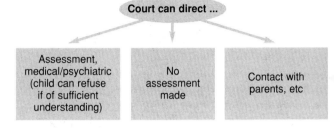

EPO gives applicant PR for duration of the order but limits its use to safeguarding the child's welfare

The authority should only remove the child from his home for as long as is necessary for the child's welfare and should return him home as soon as it is safe to do so. However, if the applicant considers that he needs to remove the child again during the existence of the order, he has the power to do so (s 44(10) and (12)).

The FLA 1996 has added s 44A to the CA 1989, which allows an exclusion requirement to be added to an EPO if the court has reasonable cause to believe that, if a person is excluded from a dwelling house in which the child lives:

- where the order is based on s 44(1)(a), (b) or (c);
- a person living in the dwelling house is to be able and willing to give to the child the care which it would be reasonable to expect a parent to give him and is to consent to the requirement.

Applying to discharge the order

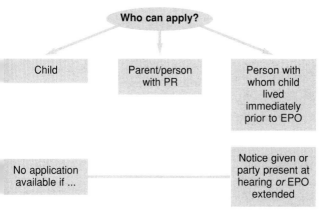

There is no appeal against an EPO, but parents may apply to discharge it after 72 hours (if the order is without notice).

Care and supervision orders

Since the Children Act 1989 came into effect, there is now only one way in which a child can be placed into the care of a local authority or be made subject to a supervision order made under that Act. This is by the applicant being able to satisfy the requirements of s 31(2) of the Act and showing that the welfare of the child demands that the order be made. Wardship can no longer be used to make a child the subject of these orders. Once an application has been made to the court under s 31(1), the court has the power to make either a care order (CO) or a supervision order (SO) if the LA has proven the 'threshold criteria'. In addition, the court can consider granting a s 8 residence order (but not in favour of the LA).

All care proceedings will commence in the Family Proceedings Court, but matters may be transferred to a designated county court or the High Court if it is considered appropriate, since all these courts have jurisdiction to deal with care matters as they fall within the definition of 'family proceedings'.

Who can apply for a care or supervision order?

Who can apply for a CO/SO?

- Local authority
- Authorised person: NSPCC

If the court is dealing with matters which are considered to be 'family proceedings' and it considers that a local authority should investigate the circumstances of the case, it has the power to direct that the authority should do so (s 37(1)).

However, if the authority carries out the investigation but decides that an application for a care order is not, in its opinion, necessary, then the court cannot require the authority to make an application. This could mean that situations may arise where children are left without measures available to safeguard their welfare, as occurred in the case of *Nottinghamshire CC v P* (1993).

A CO or SO can only be made in respect of a child who is under 17 years of age (or 16 if the child is married).

The threshold criteria

When the local authority has decided that an application is to be made, then it must be able to fulfil the requirements of s 31(2), which have become known as the 'threshold criteria'.

Both parts need to be satisfied

Significant harm + Causation:
(a) the level of care not being reasonable
or
(b) control

M v Birmingham City Council (1994)

A vital element to remember is that, even when the authority has been able to satisfy the 'threshold criteria', the court will be required to consider the contents of s 1 of the Act.

The welfare, delay and 'no order' principles must be borne in mind before the final decision is made. They form the basis of the court's decision in all 'family proceedings'.

Section 31(9) contains the definitions of the terms used in the threshold criteria:

Harm	Ill treatment or the impairment of health and development
Development	Physical, intellectual, emotional, social or behavioural development
Health	Physical or mental health
Ill treatment	Includes sexual abuse and other forms of ill treatment which are not physical

Other definitions

Significant	Considerable, noteworthy or important: *Humberside CC v B* (1993)
Care	Normal physical and emotional care that a reasonable parent would give

Test to apply to s 31(10)

When looking at the effect of any failings relating to the health and development of the child, s 31(10) states that the child in question must be judged against what can be expected of a similar child, having taken into account the characteristics of that child; that is, the court must take a subjective view of the child in question and apply an objective test when comparing him with a similar child.

When to assess the threshold criteria

The House of Lords' decision in *Re M (A Minor) (Care Order: Threshold Conditions)* (1994) settled this issue: the time when judgment about significant harm being suffered has to be made is when the local authority commences proceedings for the protection of the child, in other words, the time that the LA takes any temporary measure which may lead to a CO application being made in the future.

The question of future harm which the child is 'likely to suffer' should be judged 'on the balance of probabilities', as in *Re H and R (Child Sexual Abuse)* (1995). It is perfectly acceptable to base a finding of future risk of harm by looking at evidence of past events, even if those events did not occur within the current family grouping (*Re D* (1993)).

The court should look at all the evidence and decide whether or not the child will suffer harm in the future if no order is made. It has been held that the words should not be construed restrictively and a CO should be granted if indicated by the evidence (*Re A (A Minor) (Care Proceedings)* (1993)).

When looking at the second part of the criteria, the harm being considered must arise from the care being given by the child's parent not amounting to what would be expected from a reasonable parent; that is, an objective test applies.

However, when looking at the element of being 'beyond parental control', it need not be the parent's fault. It may be that, if the parent has tried to discipline the child but has failed, the child would then be beyond control and could be the subject of an application. The parent could ask the LA to make such an application, but it will be up to the authority to decide whether or not to do so.

How decisions on care orders will be reached

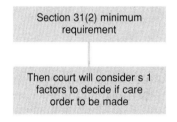

The effects of a care order

While a CO is in force in respect of the child, the LA will have parental responsibility for him (s 33).

```
LA
gets PR
```

```
Shares with parents
```

but

```
LA as senior partner can limit
parents' use of parental responsibility
*only* if necessary for child's welfare
```

Restrictions on LA – it may not:

- change the child's religion;
- agree or refuse to agree to the child's adoption;
- consent or refuse to the making of a freeing order;
- change the child's surname or remove him from the UK without the written consent of every person with parental responsibility for the child or the leave of the court.

```
CO discharges
```

```
Section 8 orders
SOs
Wardship
```

It is important to remember that the court will not interfere with the way that the local authority will implement a CO. Since it is seen that Parliament intended that local authorities should be trusted to do as they see fit when dealing with children in their care, the court, having had the opportunity to study the authority's plan when deciding to make the order, should allow the authority to manage the situation and should not attach conditions to a CO (*Re T (A Minor) (Care Order: Conditions)* (1994)). One of the difficulties that will be faced by the courts will be the interface with the European Convention on Human Rights. It can be questioned whether the lack of supervision by the court on implementation of the care plan satisfies the requirement for judicial involvement (*R v W and B* (2001)).

Parental contact with a child in care

Section 34 of the Act states that there is a statutory presumption that the authority must allow the child to have reasonable contact with certain groups of people after the granting of the order, and the authority is expected to present its proposals for contact to the court.

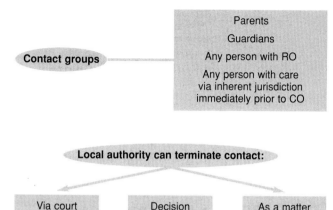

Supervision orders and their effects

An SO puts the child under the supervision of a local authority or a probation officer. The supervising body/officer does not acquire PR.

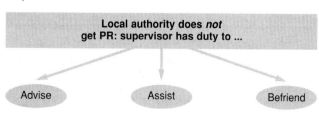

Supervisor ...

- Takes steps to give effect to the order
- Considers variation/discharge

An SO can impose obligations on a responsible person with their consent:

- Take steps to ensure child complies with directions
- Take steps to ensure child complies with requirements re medical/psychiatric examination/treatment
- Ensure child complies with directions to attend re activities

Schedule 3(4) states that an SO can require the child:

(a) to submit to a medical or psychiatric examination; and
(b) to submit to any such examination from time to time, as directed by the supervisor.

Schedule 4(4) states that no court may include such a requirement, unless satisfied that:

(a) where the child has sufficient understanding to make an informed decision, he consents to its inclusion; and
(b) satisfactory arrangements have been, or can be, made for the examination.

Supervisor can direct the child:

- To live in a certain place
- To attend activities specified in the directions
- To present himself to person(s) at places specified in the directions

Duration: one year – possible extension up to three years

Schedule 3(3) states that a supervisor does not have power to give directions in respect of medical/psychiatric examination/treatment. This is a matter for the court.

Interim care orders and supervision orders

In most cases where the LA has applied for a CO or an SO, the court will be unable to reach a conclusion as to how finally to deal with a case and may need to make an interim order until further inquiries have been made and reports submitted for its consideration. The court can also make an interim order if, in the context of private law proceedings, it has requested an investigation of the child's situation by the LA, under s 37. This will normally occur when the court feels that the child is at risk of harm if they remain with their carers without suitable input from the LA.

6 Children II

Interim orders available if:

- Care proceedings adjourned
- Direction under s 37

- s 1(2) must be considered
- Court has reasonable grounds to believe s 31(2) can be satisfied

Duration: maximum eight weeks; no limit on number made, but subsequent renewals for four weeks maximum.

The FLA 1996 has introduced s 38A into the CA 1989. This allows an exclusion requirement to be added to an interim CO if the court has reasonable cause to believe that:

◌ if a person is excluded from the child's home or prevented from entering it, the child will cease or cease to be likely to suffer significant harm;
◌ a person living in the house must be able and willing to care for the child and must consent to the requirement.

During the period of the interim CO, the court has the power to order assessments under s 38(6). While the section implies that these assessments are of the child, the House of Lords has indicated that assessment can be of the family if, by assessing, the court is then provided with all the relevant facts to make its decision. The fact that a family assessment may be expensive is irrelevant if it is necessary to the decision; the LA cannot plead poverty and hence fetter the court's discretion – *Re C (Interim Care Order: Residential Assessment)* (1997).

Discharge of a care order

The court will decide the matter on the principles contained in s 1 of the Act.

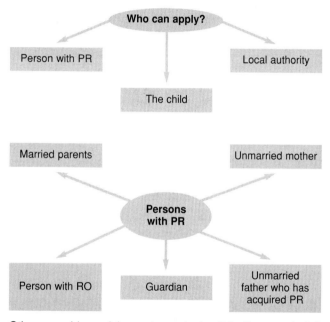

Others would need leave to apply for RO. If granted, RO would vest PR in the applicant and end the CO. If the applicant is the LA, the court may substitute an SO in place of the CO – there is no need to prove s 31(2) again. If the application is refused, no further applications may be made within six months without leave of the court.

Appointment of a children's guardian

Section 41(1) of the Act states that, in care and supervision proceedings, a children's guardian (formerly called the guardian ad litem) must be appointed to represent the child unless they are not needed to safeguard the child's interests.

The children's guardian is an independent social worker; that is, he is not employed by the local authority involved in the proceedings.

Children's guardian has duty to safeguard child's interest

- Ascertain child's understanding of the situation
- Ascertain child's wishes
- Investigate the case

Children's guardian has duty to:

- Access local authority record
- Submit report to court
- Appoint a solicitor if not done by the court

Court can consider any statement in report by children's guardian and any evidence re matters mentioned in the report considered by the court to be relevant, regardless of any act/rule of law making such evidence inadmissible

A solicitor may also be appointed by the children's guardian, unless one has already been appointed by the court. The children's guardian will give the solicitor instructions on the child's behalf unless the child has sufficient understanding to do so himself.

Wardship and inherent jurisdiction

The wardship jurisdiction of the court is used to protect the interests of children where parental responsibility for the child rests with the court. If wardship is granted, then the child will often stay with the party that made the application, but that party will not be able to take any important decision in the child's life without the consent of the court, which can also give directions to safeguard the welfare of the child (*Re S* (1967)).

The inherent jurisdiction of the High Court is the use of the power of the Crown as *parens patriae*. This stems from the duty of the Crown to protect its subjects. The inherent jurisdiction is theoretically without limit, but, in practice, limits do apply. Where the inherent jurisdiction applies to children, it gives the court the ability to exceed the powers and overrule the decisions of parents and '*Gillick* competent' children (*Re W (A Minor) (Consent to Medical Treatment)* (1993)).

The inherent jurisdiction exists independently of wardship and can be used to protect the interests of a child who has not been made a ward. It is generally used to settle a specific issue, very often a medical matter, and as it deals with issues relating to PR, overlaps with certain s 8 orders under the CA 1989, for example specific issues orders.

A very clear example occurred in the case of *Re M (A Minor) (Medical Treatment)* (1999). In this case, a 15 and a half year old girl refused to consent to a heart transplant, even though the doctors treating her considered that, without it, she would die.

The court was asked to overrule her refusal and allow the treatment to go ahead. The court followed the principle laid down in *Re W* and the treatment was carried out.

Wardship and the Children Act 1989

The CA 1989 has, as we have seen, introduced a flexible range of orders which are available to the court when dealing with 'family proceedings'. This has made the use of wardship much less likely than previously, and it will generally only be necessary in cases where the orders are unavailable or where speed is of the essence.

Private law matters

The CA 1989 has not placed any restriction on the use of wardship in private law matters. However, the wide range of powers in s 8 of the Act makes it more likely that the parties will use these orders rather than wardship.

There will be times when using wardship could be an advantage. If there is a leave requirement under the CA 1989, the use of wardship will avoid this. Also, if the element of continuing judicial control is thought to be necessary, then, again, wardship will be the better route to take (*Re G-U (A Minor) (Wardship)* (1984)).

Public law matters

Unlike private law matters, the area of public law in respect of wardship has been severely restricted by the CA 1989. Section 100(2) ensures that local authorities are no longer allowed to use wardship or the inherent jurisdiction to take children into care or make them subject to an SO.

However, there are situations where LAs are still able to use the inherent jurisdiction, albeit with the leave of the court (s 100(3)).

In order to grant leave, the court must be satisfied that:

- the result that the local authority wishes to achieve could not be achieved by the making of any other type of order which the local authority might be entitled to apply for under the statutory code; and
- there is reasonable cause to believe that, if the court's inherent jurisdiction is not exercised with respect to the child, he is likely to suffer significant harm.

Cases where such a cause has been found are where medical treatment was needed for a child who refused consent (*Re W (A Minor) (Medical Treatment: Court's Jurisdiction)* (1993)) and where publicity would be harmful to the child (*Essex CC v Mirror Group Newspapers* (1996)). Wardship is also useful where the child is over 17, since the LA cannot make an application for a CO/SO if the child is over this age and still below 18.

However, just because leave is granted, the inherent jurisdiction will not necessarily be exercised (*Essex CC v Mirror Group Newspapers* (1996)). It will still be necessary to show that significant harm is likely to occur; however, this usually causes no difficulty.

6 Children II

```
Wardship cannot be used to obtain CO/SO or PR
                    │
                    ▼
        LA must use s 31(2)
        threshold criteria for CO/SO
         │                    │
         ▼                    ▼
Child in care cannot      If warded child
be warded                 taken into care,
         │                wardship ceases
         ▼
Court cannot give local
authority PR it does not
already have
```

Wardship applications

Wardship proceedings begin with originating summons in the Family Division at the High Court: the minor is warded when summons are issued.

Usual applicants:
- LA
- Parents
- Any person with sufficient interest
- Child with/without children's guardian

Publicity

In wardship proceedings, the court has the power to make an injunction prohibiting the publication of information which is considered harmful to the child. Any order made is binding on every person who is potentially subject to the order, even though they have not been joined as a party to the proceedings.

Although the publication of information relating to proceedings before any court sitting in private is not in itself a contempt, there are exceptions to this situation, including:

- proceedings which relate to the exercise of the inherent jurisdiction of the High Court in relation to minors;
- proceedings under the CA 1989; and
- any other proceedings which relate wholly or mainly to the maintenance or upbringing of a minor.

When deciding such matters, the court will *not* regard the welfare of the child as paramount, but it will regard the child's welfare as the most important consideration. The balance that the court will seek to achieve when reaching its decision will be between the welfare of the child and the public interest (*Re H (Minors) (Injunction: Public Interest)* (1993)).

Adoption

The legislation covering adoption is contained in the Adoption Act 1976. However, the legislative provisions will be changing in the future following the implementation of the Adoption and Children Act 2002, which was granted royal assent at the end of the 2002 parliamentary session. The purpose of the Act is to increase the number of children who are adopted out of care, to ensure that adoptive parents are encouraged to come forward, to change the time frames in which an adoption order can be made, to alter the emphasis in relation to the welfare of the child, and to alter the procedural steps that must be undertaken. The basic concept of adoption will remain.

An adoption order brings a legal adoption into being and ends a natural parent's parental responsibility, vesting it in the adoptive parents (s 12(1)). It also ends any parental responsibility that any other person may have had for the child and brings to an end any order made under the CA 1989. However, such proceedings fall within the definition of 'family proceedings' and, as such, the court will be able to make use of s 8 orders in the proceedings, should they consider them necessary. This is most likely in the case of a step-parent seeking to adopt a stepchild.

Adoption agencies are responsible for arranging adoptions unless the prospective adopter is a relative or a person acting under a High Court order. Adoption agencies are run by local authorities or approved voluntary adoption societies. In practice, most local authorities run the service within their own area.

Welfare of the child

Section 6 of the Adoption Act 1976 states that:

> In reaching any decision in relation to the adoption of a child, a court or adoption agency must have regard to all the circumstances, first consideration being given to the need to safeguard and promote the welfare of the child throughout his childhood; and shall, so far as practicable, ascertain the wishes and feelings of the child regarding the decision and give due consideration to them, having regard to his age and understanding.

Thus, it must be noted that the child's welfare is not paramount but is the first consideration.

When the 2002 Act is implemented this approach will change. The child's welfare shall become the court's paramount concern, and the court will have a new statutory checklist to consider. Whilst this checklist is similar to that in the CA 1989, it has some differences. The court will need to consider:

- the child's wishes (in the light of age and understanding);
- the child's needs;
- the effect on the child of being adopted;
- age/sex/background of the child;
- any harm they have suffered/may suffer;
- the child's relevant relationships.

Who can adopt?

Joint application	Married couples both over 21 years. If one party a parent, then that person need only be over 18 years
Single application	Over 21 years. Married or single
If married and single application, must show that spouse:	Cannot be found
	Separated permanently
	Incapable of making application

The 2002 Act, somewhat controversially, has changed the law as to who can seek an adoption order. When implemented, the 2002 Act will permit heterosexual cohabiting couples and same-sex cohabiting couples to adopt as a couple, in contrast to the above where only one of the couple can adopt, with the other having to seek a joint residence order to gain any sort of PR.

Who can be adopted

Who can be adopted?

Child must be of minimum age and under 18 who is not nor has been married. Must have lived with applicants for requisite time

- Where applicant is: parent; step-parent; relative, or child has been placed with applicants by an adoption agency or the High Court (legal adoptions)
  - Child must be over 19 weeks old and have lived with applicants for preceding 13 weeks

- Other applicants (illegal adoptions)
  - Child must be over 12 months old and have lived with applicants for previous 12 months

The 2002 reforms will affect the relevant time frames indicated above. Once a child has been placed for adoption under a placement order (see below), the court will be able to make an order after the child has been with the applicant for the following times:

Applicant is an approved prospective adopter . . . . 10 weeks
Applicant is a step-parent . . . . 6 months
Applicant is a foster parent . . . . 1 year
Applicant is none of the above . . . . 5 years

Considerations for the court

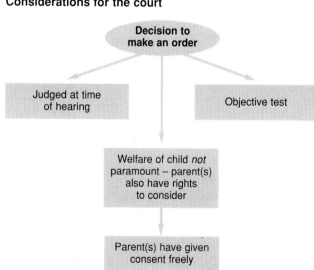

The mother of the child cannot give an effective consent to an adoption order until at least six weeks after the birth of her child (ss 16(4) and 18(4)).

The court must be satisfied that the consent is freely given, with full understanding of the situation, and is unconditional. It must be witnessed by the reporting officer, who will also provide the court with a full report on the case.

Parental agreement

Before a court can make an adoption order, it must obtain the agreement of the parents/guardian of the child.

However, there will be times when the court will consider it necessary to dispense with parental agreement.

Grounds for dispensing with parental agreement

The grounds are contained in s 16(2). They are when a parent or guardian:

- cannot be found or is incapable of giving agreement;
- is withholding his agreement unreasonably;
- has persistently failed without reasonable cause to discharge his parental responsibility for the child;
- has abandoned or neglected the child;

- has persistently ill treated the child;
- has seriously ill treated the child.

Parent cannot be found or is incapable of giving consent

In these circumstances, inquiries must be made in an effort to trace the relevant persons to give them notice of the proposed adoption. If they cannot be found, the requirement for their consent can be dispensed with. This is also permitted where their whereabouts are known but they cannot be contacted, as in *Re R (Adoption)* (1966): the parents could not be contacted due to the nature of the political regime in their country.

In *Re L (A Minor) (Adoption: Parental Agreement)* (1987), it was held that the natural mother was incapable of giving her consent as she was suffering from a mental disorder under the Mental Health Act 1983 and was unable to understand the consequences of the adoption.

Parent is withholding his agreement unreasonably

When considering this ground, the court must bear in mind that the fact that the parent does not agree with the proposed adoption will not *per se* make it unreasonable. A number of considerations must be kept in mind when deciding whether or not it is unreasonable.

The decision must be judged at the time of the hearing and an objective test used, that is, 'Would a reasonable parent withhold their consent?'. Also, it must be remembered that the child's welfare is not to be considered as paramount, as, in this situation, the parent is in danger of losing his parental responsibility and rights in respect of the child and must be able to intervene if he has reasonable grounds to do so. As such, the child's welfare is not allowed to override all other factors.

Having said that the welfare is not paramount, it must be seen as the most important factor – any reasonable parent would see it as such and would look to see if the child would benefit from adoption. If obvious advantages would arise, perhaps the parent should not withhold his consent.

However, the mere fact that a parent withholds his agreement does not make it unreasonable. There can be any number of views taken by any number of people to a given situation, and none of them need be unreasonable; they may be right or wrong but not necessarily unreasonable.

The court has to decide whether or not the decision on the case falls within this 'band' of reasonableness.

Compare the cases of *Re PA (An Infant)* (1971) and *Re D (An Infant) (Adoption: Parental Consent)* (1977).

Parent has persistently failed without reasonable cause to discharge his parental responsibility for the child

This factor includes the statutory duty on the parent to maintain the child and to give the normal love and affection expected from a parent.

Both elements of this ground must be satisfied, that is, the element of persistence and the element of 'without just cause'.

The element of 'persistence' must be seen in the sense of being permanent and complete to such a degree that there would be no advantage to the child in maintaining contact with the parent, as was held in *Re B (S) (An Infant) (No 2)* (1968), where a father had not sought access to the child for a number of years and had failed to enquire about her or to maintain her during that period. The court held that he had washed his hands of her and dispensed with his consent.

In *Re M (An Infant)* (1965), where an unmarried mother had left her child with the proposed adopters in order to conceal the birth from her parents, the court held that she had failed to carry out her parental duties 'with just cause'.

Parent has abandoned or neglected the child

'Abandoned' in this sense is equated with conduct which could render the parent liable to prosecution under the criminal law and is restrictively interpreted, as is the term 'neglected'. Because of this approach, this factor is rarely used in practice.

Parent has persistently ill treated the child

'Persistent' is treated as above, that is, permanent; and, in the case of *Re A (A Minor) (Adoption: Dispensing with Agreement)* (1981), it was held that a child who had been severely and repeatedly assaulted over a three week period had been persistently ill treated.

Parent has seriously ill treated the child

Under this ground, a single incident could lead the court to dispense with parental agreement if it is of a sufficiently serious nature, for example, an incident of sexual abuse.

Freeing for adoption

Section 18(1) of the Adoption Act 1976 allows an adoption agency to apply to the court for a 'freeing order', which declares that the child is free for adoption.

6 Children II

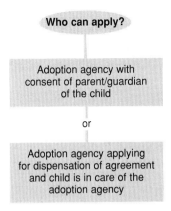

The consent of the unmarried father is not required, but the court must be satisfied that he does not intend to apply for a parental responsibility order or residence order, or that, if he did make such an application, it would be likely to be refused.

Even though a freeing order ends PR, unless a declaration is made by the former parent that he prefers not to be involved in future questions concerning the adoption, the adoption agency must inform him, within 14 days following the date 12 months after the making of the freeing order, whether the child has been adopted or placed for adoption. It must also inform him whenever the child is placed or ceases to have his home with a person with whom he has been placed, until an adoption order is made.

In such a situation, the former parent may apply for the freeing order to be revoked on the ground that he wishes to resume PR when:

- no adoption order has been made in respect of the child; and
- the child does not have his home with a person with whom he has been placed for adoption.

If the revocation is granted, it will extinguish the adoption agency's PR and revive that of the parents. Any Children Act orders extinguished by the freeing order will not be revived. However, if the child was in care prior to the freeing order, problems could arise regarding the suitability of granting full PR to the parent. In such cases, it could be made a condition of revocation that orders be made under the CA 1989 or under the court's inherent jurisdiction: *Re G (Adoption: Freeing Order)* (1997).

Changes made by the Adoption and Children Act 2002

After implementation of the 2002 Act there will be a reduction in the number of situations where the court will be able to override a parent's refusal of consent, and freeing will disappear from the process. A parent will still be required to consent, either to the placement of the child with the prospective adopters (and can give consent to the actual adoption order at this time) or to the making of a placement order. A mother will not be able to give valid consent until six weeks after the birth. The situations in which the court will be able to dispense with the parent's/parents' consent are:

- if the parent(s) cannot be found;
- if the parent(s) lack capacity;

- if it would be in accordance with the child's welfare to dispense with consent.

Freeing orders will be replaced with placement orders, which in reality will amount to the same thing. The order can be sought if the parent(s) agree to the child being placed for adoption and the child is subject to a care order, or the court is satisfied that the threshold criteria for making a care order are proven. Finally, it should be noted that the Act sets out a new regime to deal with contact with the child when placed for adoption or subject to a placement order. Contact orders under the CA 1989 will be revoked, but an application by one of the specified individuals can be made under this Act.